THE
Fright
Before
Christmas

THE
Fright
Before
Christmas

Surviving Krampus
& Other Yuletide Monsters

JEFF BELANGER

ILLUSTRATIONS BY T. REED

This edition first published in 2023 by New Page Books, an imprint of
Red Wheel/Weiser, LLC
With offices at:
65 Parker Street, Suite 7
Newburyport, MA 01950
www.redwheelweiser.com

ISBN: 978-1-63748-015-1
Library of Congress Control Number: 2023930506

Interior illustrations by Terry Reed

Book design by Sky Peck Design
Cover art created from a period Austrian Weihnachten (Christmas) card from 1898
Interior art credits on page 183
Typeset in Centaur

Printed in China
LPP

10 9 8 7 6 5 4 3 2 1

For Mom.
Christmas has no bigger fan.
Thanks for instilling in me the magic of the holiday.
And thank you for keeping Krampus away.

This humble book is my attempt to save Christmas, even if only for myself. To bring the holiday back to a time when it included everyone. I couldn't do it alone, though. I needed to summon a horde of creepy and chilling monsters to help me tell the tale of how we got to right now, and how we can return the true spirit of this creepiest of holidays. I'm forever in debt to these deadly beasties.

—Jeff Belanger

Contents

ACT THREE: REDEMPTION

Acknowledgments

No one puts a book like this together alone. I'm grateful for the team of people who caught the vision for celebrating the darker side of this spooky holiday. Thank you to my agent, Eric Myers, and to Michael Pye at New Page Books. Thank you to my editor Shana Jones for making this book better. Thank you to Kathryn Sky-Peck for turning this book into a work of art, and thank you to T. Reed for the masterful illustrations. I also appreciate the efforts of Elliot McNally at the Coca-Cola Company for allowing us to use the company's 1931 Santa Claus ad.

Thank you to my mom and dad for instilling the magic of the holiday in me as a child, and for helping to continue the traditions with my daughter. Thank you to my wife, Megan, who is always my first reader and editor, and the person who kept me sane while this book consumed me. Thank you to my daughter, Sophie, for making me laugh, and for teaching me the true meaning of the holiday from the earliest days that she gazed in wide-eyed wonder at the lights on our Christmas tree.

Thank you to my friends who are always ready to help with reading, input, or photography, especially Frank Grace, Tony Dunne, and Jane Gardner.

I'm also grateful to all of the people who spoke to me about their traditions and countries. Though their names are already mentioned in this book, thanks to Richard Sheridan and the Krampus Society of New England, *Þakka þér fyrir* to Terry Gunnell for teaching me the Icelandic ways, *met dank* to Elizabeth Koert and her mom, Mary Vallo, *merci beaucoup* to Pauline Giorgetti, thanks Raylene Ball for mummering with me, *grazie* to Frederic Berruti, and *danke* to Christoph and Katharina Rieser.

Introduction

It was a cold and cloudy Saturday in early December. Fighting the chill making its way into my bones, I was hanging holiday lights on the bushes in front of my Massachusetts home. My fingers were quickly growing numb and stiff from the bitter wind. Frustrated with untangling the string of lights I pulled from the box I tossed them in eleven months ago, I moved over to hanging a wreath on my front door.

The wreath was fake. Pretty, but artificial. There were red plastic berries, green plastic evergreens, and pinecones. The pinecones were real but coated with a plastic spray to preserve them. I have this thin crafting wire I use to attach the wreath to my brass door knocker. I caught a glimpse of my own reflection in the door knocker just as last year's rusty craft wire snapped, sending the wreath to the ground.

"Humbug!" I would have yelled in another place and time, but in this instance it was a more colorful expletive that escaped my lips—not "escaped" so much as left my mouth the way a bullet leaves a gun. I took a deep breath, my shoulders slumped, and I asked my distorted door knocker reflection: *Why?*

Why the wreath on the front door?
Why the evergreens?
Why the lights?

Why the Christmas tree?

Why Santa Claus?

Why do we spend so much time, effort, and money on this one day?

This holiday is too commercial already. Am I only contributing to the problem?

I should also point out that I'm a father and a husband. At the time of hanging these lights and decorations in the bitter cold, my daughter believed in Santa and the power of Christmas. She believed because I instilled those beliefs in her since before she could talk. Traditionally speaking, though, Christmas isn't *my* holiday. Halloween is.

I'm a paranormal guy. I've made a career out of chasing ghosts and monsters all over the world, and sharing those stories on stages, television, podcasts, and in books. I've come to enjoy the Christmas holiday because it marks the end of my busy Halloween season. But when my Christmas wreath hit the ground and I gazed at my angry, warped reflection in my door knocker, those very questions I just posed began to haunt me. Then a lyric from Andy Williams's most popular Christmas song popped into my head: "There'll be scary ghost stories, and tales of the glories of Christmases long, long ago . . ."

Scary ghost stories? I never grew up with scary ghost stories at Christmas. What was this 1963 holiday song referring to? I had to know more. But mostly, I wanted to learn how I got here on my front steps in the cold, wrestling with artificial lights and a wreath.

My research led me down a dark and sinister rabbit hole. Very soon I would learn that Halloween is just the warm-up act for the most frightening holiday of the year. Most of us know this holiday as Christmas, but it had gone by other names long before it became associated with Christians. Saturnalia. Yule. Midwinter. No matter what label you prefer, all of this fuss centers on a cosmic event that's occurred annually for billions of years no matter what you believe (or don't believe): the Winter Solstice.

The Winter Solstice is a time to be afraid. It's the shortest day of the year. The longest night. In some parts of the world, the sun doesn't rise at all. It's dark, and we have to wonder if the sun will ever return.

Put your mind back to a place just a few centuries ago in some Nordic country. Picture your small house by the edge of a forest as the Winter Solstice draws close, and you have to ask yourself: *Do I have enough food to make it through the long winter? Will my roof hold up under all of that snow? Will I keep my sanity while shut inside with little to do until spring? Can I keep my children safe? Will I find game to hunt so my family can eat? And what's that sound outside? Is it just the wind whipping through naked trees, or is that the anguished cries of angry spirits?*

You look out your window at the landscape and see that winter kills everything. The grass. The trees. The flowers. Even the ponds and lakes are frozen in an eerie stillness. It's bleak and desolate. Get caught outside unprepared, and winter will kill you too.

The Winter Solstice is a time for fear. And in the darkest corners of that fear . . . there be monsters lurking! Lethal monsters who have come to set us on the correct moral path, punish us if we need to be redirected, or murder and eat us if there's no hope for our souls.

Some of these monsters have been around for centuries. And though at times we've pushed them into the far corners of our collective psyches, these creatures have a way of hibernating until we need them again.

I'm here to both inform and warn you that they're coming back.

When I was a child, I was told I would receive sticks and coal in my stocking at Christmas if I was naughty. Sticks and coal are hardly a punishment for a year of tormenting my parents. Imagine if instead of sticks and coal, I was warned of the beasts who lurked in the shadows of December to tear me from my snuggly bed and beat me . . . or worse!

If only I had known that the Tomten had his eye on me, that the Belsnickel was ready to hit me with his switch of sticks, or that the Grýla might drag me back to her mountain lair and cook me in her stew.

Krampus, the Christmas Devil and king of the Yuletide beasts, also had his sights on me. But at least I could hear him coming with his rattling chains and bells. There are other violent and dangerous monsters from all over northern climes who have been hunting naughty children for generations. From shapeshifters to mountain trolls, to heavy-handed cohorts of Saint Nicholas, the Christmas holiday has been filled with ghosts and monsters ready to dole out punishment to those who earned it.

We *should* be scared. Most of what we know and love about this holiday was built on the back of a ghost story told by a master. None of us can forget the night Ebenezer Scrooge was haunted by old Jacob Marley, who came to warn him that the ponderous chain Scrooge was forging in life would weigh him down for all eternity if he didn't get busy doing good instead of turning inward toward his own selfishness. But, if Scrooge confronted his ghosts and demons, there may just be hope.

While there's plenty to fear during this dark and cold time of year, at the heart of that fear lies hope that, like Scrooge, we can all change in a single night if given the right motivation. If you can't find it in your heart to be kind and charitable for its own sake . . . then allow me to introduce you to some hordes of Yuletide beasts who are ready to set you straight by any means necessary during a dark and frightening time fraught with danger.

But first, let's take a moment to consider: How did we get here?

ACT ONE

HOPE

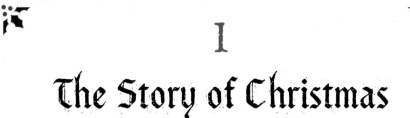

I

The Story of Christmas

hen we hear the words "Christmas story," many, if not most, people think of a meager manger in Bethlehem where we're told a baby was born to be a Savior. In the modern Christian tradition, Christmas, and the period of Advent that precedes it, is a celebration of the birth of Christ; it's a season of hope.

I mean no disrespect to my Christian friends, but from a historical perspective, a religious perspective, a folkloric, and even a biblical perspective, this holiday has little to do with the birth of Jesus.

Christmas is a story of hope . . . and fear

The *real* story behind Christmas—the tale of how we got to what has always been a manufactured event—is purely astronomical: the Winter Solstice. The true meaning of this holiday is a celebration of all humankind and of nature. It's about hope and fear. Darkness and light. This book is a journey of how we have managed the most terrifying time of year. In Act One, we'll set the historical stage for this Midwinter holiday and examine the ways our ancestors prepared for the darkest and coldest of days; how they found hope in the blackest corners of a frozen landscape. From Saturnalia festivals that turned society on its head if only for a few days, to Yule traditions of honoring the sacred and powerful evergreen and its ability to ward off angry spirits. These parties were life-affirming and offered a chance to reconnect and bond with family and neighbors. Then there's our reverence for the miracles and generous gifts of Saint Nicholas of Myra—showing believers that the impossible can happen in an instant if you have faith. In Act Two, we'll attempt to survive the hordes of monsters lurking during this otherwise festive season. Monsters who, though they may be lethal, ultimately offer us a chance at redemption. And redemption is what we'll find in Act Three, thanks to some powerful and frightening spirits who have come to save us from ruin.

As the song says, "You better watch out, you better not cry . . ." Because the consequences during this time of year are dire. And I'm going to tell you why.

❄ ❄ ❄

In the Bible, the birth of Jesus does not get a lot of ink. That's not a mistake. First, *everyone* is born. It's not a big deal. (I beg forgiveness from every person who has ever birthed a child. Of course it's a very big deal when you are doing the pushing, but considering there are eight billion of us on the Earth as of this writing, it's not quite fair to call childbirth a miracle anymore.) Jesus was born a commoner. Commoners back then didn't track their birthdays—only royalty did that. All of Christianity doesn't hinge on the birth of Jesus. The religion hinges on the belief that Jesus died and was resurrected. The Easter story is the big one with plenty of ink in the Bible.

Still, the Bible does give us a few clues as to when Jesus was born. Jesus was born in Bethlehem in Judea, during the time of King Herod.

King Herod ruled from 37 BCE until his death in 4 BCE, so we would place the birth of Jesus around 4 BCE, give or take a few years. Which I know is a head-scratcher, because I always assumed BC ended and AD began with the birth of Jesus in the year 0. The reason for the discrepancy is because in the sixth century, a monk named Dionysius Exiguus proposed that the Christian era should begin with the birth of Jesus. Many fellow Christians agreed, but mistakes were made.

While adding up Roman history, Exiguus missed the four-year reign of Emperor Octavian. The calendar has been off ever since. Too late now. Time and tide wait for no one.

As to what time of year Jesus was born, the Bible gives us one clue. It can be found in Luke 2:8–9:

> And there were shepherds living out in the fields nearby, keeping watch over their flocks at night. An angel of the Lord appeared to them, and the glory of the Lord shone around them, and they were terrified.

In the region of Bethlehem, which sits just south of Jerusalem in Israel, shepherds would sit out with their flock at night between spring months and as late as October. After that, it's too cold to be out all night. Which means, according to the Bible, the only months we can rule out for the birth of Jesus are roughly November through April.

Before you cry heretic, please understand I don't always celebrate my birthday on the actual day either. Sometimes we wait for the weekend, or sometimes I get together with my sister, whose birthday is three weeks after mine. There are no rules as to when the day must be commemorated. So how did we land on December 25?

For that, we must thank the Roman emperor Constantine.

When Constantine began his reign in 306 CE, he was old enough to have lived through the persecution of early Christians. He was also young enough to see Christianity expanding, because the idea that one could be born common and still receive great rewards in heaven sounded like a sweet deal. As Christianity grew in popularity and numbers, the ruling class had a choice: continue to persecute, which would only solidify the opposition, or embrace it.

Emperor Constantine and the Council of Nicaea. The burning of Arian books is illustrated below. From MS CLXV, Biblioteca Capitolare, Vercelli, a compendium of canon law produced in northern Italy ca. 825.

Constantine converted to Christianity in 312 AD, after a vision he experienced at the Battle of the Milvian Bridge. Though other emperors and generals had attempted to legalize Christianity, if for no other reason than to try and recruit this growing group into military service, it was Constantine's Edict of Milan in 313 that set the wheels in motion to unify Rome under one religion. This edict meant Christianity was now legal to practice, and Constantine ordered that any Christian property that had been confiscated had to be returned, and that the harmed should be compensated.

The Edict of Milan did *not* forbid other faiths. Far from it. All gods and beliefs were respected, but each belief system needed a kind of license in order to meet legally. The Edict of Milan made Christian meetings legal.

To cement the political potency of the faith, Constantine then also called the Council of Nicaea in 325 AD in what is now İznik, Turkey, with the goal of unifying Christianity. Specifically, the council wanted to address a controversy of Arianism, which held that Christ was not divine, but was a man born like any other—an idea that most bishops found heretical. Out of this meeting, these early leaders deemed that Christ was indeed divine, and that Easter was the most important holiday to the church—the crucifixion and resurrection are the foundation the religion is built upon. One of the bishops in attendance at the Council of Nicaea was a man named Nicholas, the Bishop of Myra. More on him soon.

Yet during this time period of solidifying Christianity, Saturnalia—a raging Pagan party meant to honor the harvest and turn society upside-down for a week—was still wildly popular. To try and stop this Pagan festival would have been political suicide. But if Christianity was going to be the official religion of Rome, Jesus Christ must be sold to the masses. If Jesus was not just a king, but the King of kings, he needed a birthday, as all royalty does.

In the Julian calendar, December 25 marks the festival of Sol Invic-tus—the sun god. December 25 is also the day that marks the Winter Solstice in the Julian calendar. It's the day the sun god begins his return to the world. The debaucherous good time of Saturnalia runs from Decem-ber 17 to 23, and then you've got this other Pagan festival of Sol Invic-tus two days later. Constantine, a logical man when it came to ruling the masses, thought it fitting to announce the birth of Jesus Christ would be celebrated on December 25 on the Winter Solstice. Many Romans were already celebrating the rebirth of the sun; now the day would celebrate the birth of the son of God. Saturnalia was still legal and celebrated, and then they tacked on another day to celebrate at the end of the six days. The party rolled on.

No formal edict survives regarding a declaration concerning Decem-ber 25; however, the furthest back this holiday appears on the calendar is the year 336 AD, so credit is given to Constantine because he was in charge. From that point on, most of the Christian world accepted Decem-ber 25 as the birthday of Jesus and thus Christmas.

The real star of the Christmas show was born centuries after Jesus, and just a few hundred miles to the north. His name is Saint Nicholas of Myra. Name sounds familiar, right? We'll get to him soon. But first, we'll go all the way back to the very beginning of this dark holiday.

2

The Winter Solstice

hy are we sitting by the fireplace with hot chocolate while holiday music fills our ears, as twinkling lights on the Christmas tree illuminate our living rooms, while Jack Frost nips the noses of those still outside in the cold? The answer lies in the backstory. We have to go as far back as humanly possible and retrace the steps to this point.

In northern climates, we live in three seasons: spring, summer, and fall. But we *survive* the winter. Though today we can turn up our thermostats and shop anytime for foods that never would have been available to our great-great-great-grandparents out of season, we still have to face bleak winters fraught with cold temperatures, seasonal affective disorder (SAD), snow delays and cancellations, winter colds and flu, and all of the other challenges winter can throw our way.

Winter was truly a perilous beast.

But think back just a few centuries, and winter was truly a perilous beast, staring us down each year, asking us to test our mettle and our ability to prepare for the harshest of conditions. Run out of food or fuel . . . you die. If your home collapses under the weight of the snow, leaving you without shelter . . . you die. If you can't find game to hunt to supplement your diet . . . you die. Get lost outside in a snowstorm . . . you die. Winter is the season of fear. It's dark, cold, and dangerous. We have to be prepared.

Why does this frightening and frigid event occur each year? We all live on this big blue-and-green ball called Earth that's hurtling through space and time at thousands of miles per hour. The planet leans on its axis as it makes an elliptical orbit around our sun. When the pole that's closest to where you are leans furthest from the sun, it's the Winter Solstice. When that pole leans closest toward the sun, it's the Summer Solstice, and the halfway points make it either the Spring or Fall Equinox. In the northern hemisphere, the Winter Solstice takes place typically on December 21 or 22 each year at a precise moment when the planet reaches its maximum tilt away from the sun.

Around the world, most significant religious holidays are tied to one of these four major seasonal events: winter, spring, summer, and fall. Or the halfway point between each of those seasons. The Pagan calendar, for example, celebrates Yule on the Winter Solstice, Imbolc on February 1, Ostara on the Spring Equinox, Beltane on May 1, Litha on the Summer Solstice, Lughnasadh on August 1, Mabon on the Autumn Equinox, and Samhain on November 1.

If you look at the Western calendar with its heavy Christian influence, you'll see many of the biggest dates fall pretty close to some of these major seasonal moments. Christmas is December 25 (just a few days after the Solstice), Groundhog Day is February 2, Easter falls close to the Spring Equinox, May Day is May 1, Midsummer is the Summer Solstice, and Halloween is October 31.

Our ancient ancestors had to know what to expect in order to survive. When humans were hunters and gatherers, they had to know when to move to warmer, drier, or wetter places to make it to the next season. Then, about twelve thousand years ago when humankind decided to put down roots and try their hand at farming, they had to understand and know the seasons better than they ever had before. Because it truly became a matter of life and death. Plant seeds at the wrong time, harvest at the wrong time, and it can mean curtains for you, your family, and everyone who depends on you. Plus, if you're going to live in harsh climates, you must have the ability to store enough food to get you through to the growing season again.

If you happen to live far enough north—specifically, above the Arctic Circle at 66.5 degrees north latitude—on the Winter Solstice, the sun won't rise at all. It's Polar Night. The sun is gone, and you may fret wondering if it will ever return.

There are parts of Alaska, Canada, Greenland, Iceland, Norway, Sweden, Finland, and Russia that experience this long darkness each Winter Solstice. It's no surprise that many of the monsters who lurk during the Yuletide season hail from these regions.

Farming is the very reason for all of this fuss and all of these monsters. The Winter Solstice is also called Midwinter, because the harvest ends by the half-holiday that is November 1. The sun is retreating until it reaches its lowest point on the Winter Solstice. After that, though cold days are ahead, the sun will start to return until it's time for the planting season again.

Something primal takes over when we're faced with unnatural cold and darkness. There's an understanding that fight or flight can occur at any moment. We're on edge. We've just witnessed winter's harsh hand kill everything in the landscape and turn it white or frozen solid. So what do we do when facing down this dreadful season and its promise of death? When we're not sure if we'll make it to spring or even tomorrow?

We party.

3

Saturnalia

n my experience, the only thing better than a party that rages all day and all night is a party that rages for a week. The Pagan celebration of Saturnalia honors the god Saturn, who is the Roman god of agriculture, time, abundance, and wealth. If you farm, a good harvest means all of those things for you and your family. In the region around Rome, there was no bigger party than Saturnalia.

Saturnalia takes place each December starting on December 17. Back then, Romans used the Julian calendar, which recognized the Winter Solstice on December 25.

The festival was first described in the fifth century BCE by the writer Macrobius, but there's evidence it had been around long before it was written down. What started as a one-day festival morphed into a three-day party, until it capped out at a week, because when something is good, more of it must be better. Which makes sense because if one had to describe Saturnalia using only one word, "excess" is a solid fit.

Saturnalia is a time to celebrate the previous season's harvest and to honor the god Saturn for his blessings. Work stops. Schools, businesses, and courts close their doors for the duration of the festival where social norms are tossed aside. For this week, servants get away with behavior that wouldn't be tolerated the rest of the year. They can say and do what they like (mostly)—living like a court jester if only for a few days. Masters dine with and serve their servants, people dress in festive clothes, men may dress as women, women dress as men, or they don wild costumes. There are feasts, singing, music, parties, sex, gambling, and gifts exchanged.

Romans decorated their homes with wreaths and greenery. A common Saturnalia gift was a *cerei*, which is a tapered wax candle. Lighting the candle signifies light returning after the Winter Solstice. In Roman households, each family may choose a pretend king, or *Saturnalicius princeps*, who leads the Saturnalia celebrations for the home. Sometimes this mock king

A 17th-century oil painting by Jan van Dalen depicting the Roman god of wine Bacchus (Kunsthistorisches Museum, Vienna). That holly wreath will show up again and again in modern depictions of Father Christmas.

"Merry Christmas!" *from the* Illustrated London News, *December 25, 1847.*
A debaucherous depiction of Christmas festivities.

is chosen by whoever discovers the coin baked into a cake, or sometimes you just have that one cousin you know would make things the liveliest. Also referred to as the "Lord of Misrule," this mischief maker may insult houseguests while dressed in outlandish clothing. Chaos is the order of the day during Saturnalia, but all in good fun.

There's a saying about idle hands doing the devil's work. Late December into January marks the most idle time of the year for most farmers. Their harvest is finished. They've made the wine and beer, and now it's ready. Animals have been slaughtered, because their meat will keep longer in the colder months. But still, now is a good time to feast on fresh meat, wine, and beer. And with very few farm chores to manage, they have time to party and cut loose.

While servants becoming the masters may seem like a bad idea on the surface, it soon became obvious to the ruling class that Saturnalia was a kind of steam valve. If you've been especially tough on some of your servants, *now* is the time to offer gifts, gratitude, and fine food. Take care of them during Saturnalia, and they may forgive you for a year of abuse. They may stick around for another year all because they were taken care of during this highest of holidays.

As with any holiday, it evolves and morphs to meet the needs of the times, the culture, and the region where it's celebrated. Traditions and foods related to that holiday are based on a mix of climate, religion, government, and the influence of other cultures. A holiday has many parents. Saturnalia fit the time, space, and climate of Rome. But if we head north to more frigid temperatures and shorter days, this time of year takes on an icy veneer.

4

Yule

ear the Arctic Circle, as the Winter Solstice approaches, the world turns white and grinds to a frozen halt. Winter's hand moves across the landscape, icing ponds and lakes and even some streams and rivers. Spring's flowers are a distant memory, the grasses turn brown and then die, and even the trees lose their leaves and now stand naked and skeletal—seemingly dead. And what's that sound? That high-pitched shriek coming from the forest? Is it just the wind whistling and whipping through those bare trees, or is it the cries of the spirits of those who fell to the Norse god Odin?

Winter's icy hand moves across the landscape.

When faced with all the fear this season brings, the Nordic people knew they better squeeze in one big party before they were stuck inside. They call this Solstice party Yule, from the Norse word *hweol*, meaning wheel. The Norse believed the sun was a wheel of fire that rolls toward the Earth, causing summer, and then the wheel rolls away again, causing winter.

As our Nordic ancestors gazed out on this bleak and dangerous world that had frozen around them, they noticed that some trees and bushes *don't* lose their leaves: evergreens. Those piney needles can stand up to winter's coldest temperatures. Clearly they must be imbued with some kind of magical qualities. So the evergreen was revered.

Should their hunters make a kill, they may drape the entrails of the fallen animal around a nearby evergreen as an offering. The bloody, dripping intestines and guts of the animal make a macabre garland that lingers until it's picked clean by other animals and birds who also must survive this

Danish boy carrying a church in the bleak landscape. Holiday postcard illustrated by Jenny Nystrom, 1910.

harshest of seasons. (Think about *that* the next time you drape strings of popcorn and cranberries around your Christmas tree.)

To protect their homes, the locals cut branches off the evergreens and placed them over doors and windows, believing that the magical, prickly needles of the branches would keep the angry spirits outside. Inside they lit candles to illuminate the long, dark night. Those lights cast a glow from their windows, serving as a beacon to both kith and kin.

Like their Roman neighbors to the south, the Nordic people also threw parties celebrating the bounty of the harvest and the fact that the wine and mead were now ready to consume. At their Yule feasts, they would consume fresh meats and pass the drinking horn—a hollowed-out animal horn used not just for consuming libations but *any* ritualistic liquid—drinking from the same cup signifying that they're all equals now.

During our modern holidays, when you mention the Yule log, many people think of an elaborate chocolate cake and frosting confection rolled to look like a small wooden log. Its origins lie in an actual tree that created both a year of magic and an incredible fire hazard.

The original Yule log was an entire tree, carved with symbols, doused with wine or ale as an offering, fed into the hearth tip-first, and pushed in deeper all day long as it burned. The ashes were considered sacred and used for rituals throughout the coming year, and just enough of the log was saved to ignite next year's tree—signifying an endless connection to the past.

As the world turned modern, dragging an entire tree into your home to burn it became impractical. So the tree shrank to a log, but the idea was still there. Greater New York City–area Christmas fans may recall the burning of the Yule log reached a kitsch pinnacle on December 24, 1966, when television station WPIX in New York filmed a burning Yule log in a fireplace decked out for Christmas. Throughout Christmas Eve and into

From The Book of Christmas *by Thomas Kibble Hervey, 1836. A very Odin-like Father Christmas shown riding a Yule goat (reminiscent of Saturnalia's capricornius), carrying a wassail bowl.*

Christmas morning of 1966, WPIX played video of this burning log set to holiday music. The actual video was only seven minutes long, and then it would loop and start over, while distant ancestors of the Nordic people living in the WPIX viewing area raised a plastic cup of eggnog to the television screen and wondered where that empty feeling inside of them was coming from.

From the people who gave us Yule, we also get the mistletoe—its pearly white berries said to be the tears of the goddess Frigg who wept over her dead son, Baldur. Her love and grief resurrected Baldur, who had been poisoned by mistletoe, so Frigg decreed that no violence could ever come to anyone who stood under the mistletoe. Just a kiss as a token of affection.

So many of our current Christmas traditions can trace their roots to the Norse people. Deeper meaning and a connection to something primal can be found in every slice of Yule log cake, in every holiday cookie, or even under that plastic mistletoe you hang in your doorway—because who couldn't use extra kisses? From displaying the sacred evergreen, to lighting holiday lights, to making an effort to treat each other as equals during this dangerous time; we party, feast, and exchange gifts because I know if my roof collapses, my family might be seeking shelter with yours. And if your roof collapses under all of that snow, I must do the same for you.

5

Saint Nicholas

anta Claus has his own backstory, one that's been blended and combined with someone named Nicholas who hails from the land of Myra, which is modern-day Turkey. In the United States, we use the names Saint Nicholas, Father Christmas, and Santa Claus interchangeably. Not so in Europe. In Europe, Santa Claus is the guy who comes down the chimney on December 24/25. Saint Nicholas is a man born in Myra's coastal city of Patara around 280 CE. For the rest of our creepy holiday journey, I will also distinguish between Saint Nicholas and Santa Claus. If they weren't two different people in your head before, please take a moment to split them apart now. We'll get to Santa Claus later, but first there was Nicholas.

Born into a wealthy Christian family, Nicholas had privilege and received the finest education available. Sadly, he was orphaned at a young age and then raised in a monastery. As an adult, he became a priest—a very wealthy priest who inherited all of his parents' money. But Nicholas had no need for many material things. What brought him joy was giving his money away to those who needed it.

There's a story of a widowed man with three daughters who fell on hard times. With no dowry, the man considered selling his daughters into prostitution in order to make ends meet. Nicholas tossed three bags of gold through the man's window to anonymously help—three sacks of gold to three grateful daughters who now had dowries.

And then there were the miracles.

The earliest miracle story associated with young Nicholas involved him walking through town to study with his teacher. Nick passed a poor woman with a withered hand. He approached the woman, laid his hand upon her, prayed, made the sign of the cross, and her hand miraculously healed to its former self.

Another story told of Nicholas is that he once sailed to the Holy Land. During the voyage, a mighty storm broke out around the ship. Unfazed, Nicholas knelt and prayed, and the storm subsided, to the wonder of all the sailors.

His spirit of generosity grew as he tossed more gold coins through open windows, or helped others in need, whether they were widows, the destitute, or orphans like himself. Devoutly Orthodox, Nicholas quickly ascended the ranks within the church.

After the death of the Bishop of Myra, Nicholas was promoted to the highest church office in the region. On the day of his consecration as bishop, a young mother was home bathing her infant in a pot being warmed by the fire below. When the cathedral bells rang, calling everyone to the special church service for Nicholas, being a very good Christian (and *not* a very attentive mother), the woman ran for the church service, completely forgetting her baby in the pot over the fire.

After the consecration service ended, the woman returned home to find her kitchen filled with smoke. Suddenly remembering she left her baby over the fire, she ran to the hearth expecting to find an overcooked infant. Yet there her baby was, sitting up and smiling, unharmed. This would-be mother of the year thanked both God and the influence of the new Bishop Nicholas for the miracle of sparing her child's life.

There's also the tale of a cannibal butcher, a crowd favorite when sharing stories of Saint Nicholas. One day, three young children were lost and hungry, when they spotted a butcher shop with light coming from within. The children stepped into the butcher shop announcing their predicament.

Could the butcher please offer them some food and a place to rest until morning, when they could find their way home?

The butcher gazed around his shop at the near-empty counters. He'd been short on meat to sell, which is troublesome for any butcher. That's when the proprietor got an idea . . . an awful idea. He welcomed the children inside, then produced his sharpest knife and cut them into pieces, placing their meat into a salting tub to sell to his customers.

In his travels soon after, Bishop Nicholas found himself drawn to this butcher shop. Nicholas walked into the building and sensed something was very wrong. He spied the large salting tub, observed the meat, and immediately knew not just *what* that was, but *who* that was. Nicholas placed his hand on the salting tub, prayed to God, and commanded, "Rise up, children." With that, the children were made whole and alive once again, and they were soon reunited with their families. (Don't forget this meaty story . . . it will come up again later.)

As bishop, Nicholas founded a poorhouse and a hospital, and he continued helping families and those in need. He traveled the countryside, casting out demons when necessary and sharing his wealth. His spirit of generosity and religious devotion made him a favorite of the people.

Nicholas died December 6, 343 AD. But his story didn't end that day. Nicholas's bones were interred in a church in Myra (present-day Demre, Turkey), where he lay for more than seven centuries—all the while, his legend was growing and spreading. The people (but not the church) began calling him *Saint* Nicholas soon after his death as stories of his miracles spread. Over the centuries, he became one of the most popular Christian figures behind Jesus, Mary, and Joseph. At one point, more churches were named after Nicholas than any of the apostles. Eventually, centuries later, even the Catholic Church officially recognized *Saint* Nicholas. They had no choice.

Christmas Greetings.

Vintage St. Nicholas Christmas postcard from late 19th-century Victorian England.

In the year 1087, holy relics were all the rage. During this year, thieves from Bari, Italy, broke into Nicholas's crypt and stole his bones for their basilica back home, where many believe his bones still reside.

However, there are those in Venice who claim traders from their city stole the bones of Nicholas in 1099. There's another claim that Norman crusaders stole the saint's bones and brought them to Kilkenny, Ireland. But the controversy doesn't end there. In October of 2017, archaeologists in Turkey explored the church in Demre and claimed that if bones were stolen in 1087 or 1099, they stole the wrong person. So maybe the mortal remains of Saint Nicholas are right where they were left.

In 2017, Father Dennis O'Neill of St. Martha of Bethany Church in Illinois claimed he had a piece of the pelvic bone of Saint Nicholas. Father O'Neill said the bone fragment could be traced back to Lyon, France. The church in Bari still has some bone fragments they claim belong to Nicholas. One of those bones is part of the left ilium, which is the upper part of the pelvis. Father O'Neill's fragment is from the lower left part of a pelvic bone. When researchers from the University of Oxford carbon-dated O'Neill's bone fragment, they found it dated to the fourth century. So, it's the right time period. It could even be from the same skeleton in Bari, if those bones were indeed Nicholas of Myra.

No matter where his mortal remains lie—whether Italy, Ireland, Turkey, or Illinois (or all of the above)—it's the story of Nicholas that matters more than his old bones. His story is what millions and then billions of people have connected to. Nicholas became the patron saint of sailors, merchants, archers, children, brewers, pawnbrokers, and students.

From the eleventh century on, news of Saint Nicholas's miracles spread throughout Western Europe. And what's not to love? A rich guy who gave it all away to those in need? A person to calm stormy seas for sailors with just a prayer? Someone who could raise the dead and help unfit parents not absentmindedly kill their own? He's the saint parents everywhere needed. And many parents prayed to him when their children were sick or missing.

Throughout Europe, Saint Nicholas was (and still is) celebrated each year on the anniversary of his death on December 6 as Saint Nicholas Day. His spirit of generosity continued, even amplified in the afterlife. During the Protestant Reformation of 1517, Martin Luther and his colleagues tried to do away with saints entirely. But Nicholas persevered. The public refused to let him go. With this Yuletide figure competing for our sacred attention, it's no wonder religious leaders tried to shut down the whole damn Christmas thing.

ACT TWO

FEAR

6

The Christmas Lights Go Out

PUBLICK NOTICE

The Observation of CHRISTMAS having been deemed a Sacrilege, the exchanging of Gifts and Greetings, dressing in Fine Clothing, Feasting and similar Satanical Practices are hereby

FORBIDDEN

with the Offender liable to a Fine of FIVE SHILLINGS

s they were with most things joyous, it was the Puritans of New England who were the real buzz-kills of Christmas.

Remnants of Saturnalia survived for many centuries. As it traveled outside of Rome, it was adopted, adapted, even Christianized at times, but to Christian religious leaders, its Pagan roots shined through no matter how you dressed it or undressed it (or cross-dressed it). The god Saturn revealed himself in the abundance, the excess, the songs, and the merrymaking. Some leaders figured it was bad enough we'd named the best day of the week (Saturday, *duh*) after Saturn ... did he need to take over this non-holiday too? So in 1647, the Puritan-led English Parliament banned the celebration of Christmas altogether.

Drunken parties were getting out of hand.

There's no biblical reference to celebrating the birth of Jesus, they reasoned correctly. And these drunken parties were getting out of hand. In 1644, Parliament declared December 25 should be a day of fasting and repentance—to atone for centuries of sin, I suppose. And Parliament made a point to hold session on December 25 each year.

That was all well and good for the extreme sect of Christians who had taken over the government, but for the working-class people who adored all the ways they'd celebrated this time of year, this would not stand. Many tried to make legal appeals to Parliament to reverse this course, and in some towns, people took to the streets to riot in protest.

In Boston, the Puritan-controlled government—which was really an extension of England's Parliament—banned the practice of celebrating Christmas in 1659. The notice read,

The Observation of Christmas having been deemed a Sacrilege, the exchanging of Gifts and Greetings, dressing in Fine Clothing, Feasting and similar Satanical Practices are hereby FORBIDDEN. With the Offender liable to a Fine of Five Shillings.

Satanical!? Five shillings in 1659 would equate to about three days' wages for a skilled tradesperson. In short, the fine would hurt.

This war on Christmas continued for decades, until 1660, when the English monarchy was restored, and King Charles II decreed: Let there be Christmas once again.

Over in Boston, the ban held until 1681, when it was lifted by order of the king who had recently dissolved Parliament. Still, even after the Christmas ban was officially lifted, people weren't necessarily free to party once again. Damage was done. Though they couldn't fine you for celebrating, they could look down their puritanical noses at you all December long and into January. They could shun you and make your life difficult. Christianity was *not* giving up its war on Christmas so easily.

The Puritans saw Christmas as a time for the rabble to indulge in booze, debauchery, and sex! How did they know about the sex? Math became the dead giveaway. As Stephen Nissenbaum points out in his book, *The Battle for Christmas*:

Social historians have discovered that the rate of premarital pregnancies in New England began to climb early in the eighteenth century, and that by mid-century it had skyrocketed. (In some New England towns almost half the first children were born less than seven months after their parents' marriage.) What makes the demographic data especially interesting is that this sexual activity had a seasonal pattern to it: There was a "bulge" in the number of births in the months of September and October—meaning that sexual activity peaked during the Christmas season.

The general public didn't seem to care so much about what you called this time of year, whether Saturnalia, Yule, Midwinter, or Christmas—they just knew what it meant: parties, drinking, feasts, sex, gifts, and fun. The Puritans declared a culture war on this holiday and did everything in their power to shut it down from the pulpit.

Imagine you're a New England Puritan sitting in church as Cotton Mather (of 1692 Salem witch trials fame) preached his 1712 Christmas sermon:

> That the Feast of Christ's Nativity is spent in Reveling. Dicing, Card-ing, Masking, and in all Licentious Liberty, for the most part, as tho' it were some Heathen Feast, of Ceres, or Bacchus. Yea, the zealous Martyr Latymer complained. That Men dishonor Christ more in the Twelve Days of Christmas, than in all the twelve Months of the Year besides . . . We lay the Charges of God upon you; That if any People take this Time, for any thing of a Riotous Tendency, you do not asso-ciate with them, in such Ungodliness . . . Can you in your Conscience think, that our Holy Savior is honored, by Mad Mirth, by long Eating, by hard Drinking, by lewd Gaming, by rude Reveling?

To the Puritan leadership, the most troublesome part of Christmas was this homage to Pagan roots. Misrule was what the holiday was all about. The notion that the working class should be welcomed at the tables of the gentry was preposterous! The Puritans couldn't stop Christmas, they couldn't control it, and they couldn't officially ban it, but from the pulpit they could threaten their congregations with dire consequences for indulging in festivities that their ancestors had celebrated for thousands of years. These were not good times for preachers to accuse you of being in league with the Devil. You could lose everything based on these kinds of accusations.

By the mid-1700s, premarital sex and a higher birthrate were statistical proof that Puritans were losing their culture war on Christmas. And Christmas, with all of its *satanical* practices, could *not* be defeated. However, the holiday was successfully suppressed to the point where it was not much of a thing in the United States. In Boston, for example, Christmas wasn't an officially recognized holiday until 1856. And even then, it still wasn't really celebrated like we know it today. However, some ghosts soon arrived in town that would change everything. But long before there were ghosts, there were monsters. By the mid-nineteenth century, the date of December 25 was catching on throughout the world as Christmas Day. But how to celebrate it was still a new idea—not yet fully formed.

However, the Feast of Saint Nicholas Day on December 6 had been well established for centuries in Europe. If December 6 belonged to Saint Nicholas . . . December 5 belonged to something much darker and more sinister.

As night fell on December 5, beware. If you'd been bad . . . your life could be in mortal danger.

7

Krampus

If you're a less-than-perfect child, and you've been told the tales, then December 5 is circled several times in red on your calendar. This is the big day. If you survive to see December 6, it means you behaved well enough to warrant gifts from Saint Nicholas. But . . . if on the fifth of December you hear rattling chains or bells coming toward your bedroom door during that long, dark, silent, deadly night . . . it's too late. Krampus has arrived.

Krampus is a monster.

He's covered in fur but stands erect on his cloven hooves—though sometimes he has one cloven hoof and one human-like foot—a nod to his demonic origins. Two devil horns sit atop his head, and a long, forked, red tongue juts out of his mouth like a serpent. He's wrapped in chains and carries a sack or a basket that he fills with every naughty child he can find. He scoops up the screaming brats, stuffs them into his sack, and carries them back to his mountain lair where he kills them and eats them. Come Saint Nicholas Day, all of the naughty children of the world are dead, so Saint Nicholas is free to bring gifts to all of the good girls and boys because good children are all that's left.

I didn't know about Krampus when I was a child. At that time, Krampus had been pushed to the far recesses of popular culture. Though he was gone, he was not completely forgotten. There were shadows of him lurking—a different name, a slightly different look. But when I think back, maybe a version of Krampus *was* there in my childhood. Back then we called him the Grinch. Covered in fur, angry, lived in a mountain lair, the fur on top of his head would occasionally curl into the shape of horns.

Vintage Krampus postcard from the late 19th-century.

6. December

Nikolaus und Krampus. Vintage postcard.

There's no doubt that Krampus inspired Dr. Seuss when he published *How the Grinch Stole Christmas* back in 1957.

Some have called Krampus the Christmas Devil, or the antagonist to Saint Nicholas, but that's not true. Krampus and Saint Nicholas are cohorts. The original bad cop/good cop. Krampus handles the dirty work while Saint Nicholas keeps his hands clean. Though it's difficult to give Krampus an exact birth date, we can trace his evolution.

Greek mythology holds the earliest roots of Krampus. The god Pan was depicted as a half man, half beast, complete with two cloven hooves and legs like a goat. Atop his head are the familiar goat horns. Pan is the god of the wild, of shepherds and flocks, and he plays his familiar flute, making him a favorite of musicians. It's from Pan we get the word "panic."

He's got the look, but that's about it. Pan doesn't deliver justice to the naughty. Though the empire that once celebrated Pan fell, Pan survived at least in art and concept. His influence is still felt many centuries later.

From here we need to travel in time to the Middle Ages and early Renaissance period. This is a time when the church began its obsession with the Devil. The Devil got very little ink in the Old Testament. One makes assumptions that the serpent in the Garden of Eden was the Devil, but it's never explicitly stated. In the Old Testament, there's simply the opposer to God. There's no physical description of the Devil in the Bible, nor are there any details on where he lives. Most of what we think we know about the Devil comes from art and literature created centuries after the Bible.

The Christian concept of the Devil is a mixture of many influences. Ancient Babylonian texts featured nasty, winged demons named Lilitu that flew through the air, seduced men, and attacked women and young children. The Jewish tradition features Lilith, Adam's first wife. In that tradition, Lilith represents lust and rebellion—traits that would be incorporated into the Christian Devil. Then there's Beelzebub, a deity from Canaan, whose name translates to "Lord of the Flies."

When the church began commissioning painters and sculptors to depict the Devil, they gave artists a lot of leeway in their interpretations, so long as the depiction was horrible and frightening. Most of the populace at this time was illiterate, but they understood imagery. The Devil had to look familiar but awful. Pan was familiar. He'd been around for many centuries. Add elements of demons from other belief systems and stories, give him character traits in opposition to the church's teachings, and artists got to work creating horror masterpieces. And why did the church commission and display these works? Because it put butts in church pews and offered them tools to control the population.

Just like today, we can't look away from negative and scary things. If the promise of God's reward wasn't enough to keep you in line, then perhaps the fear of the Devil's wrath would do it. Krampus emerged from this Christian quagmire of devils and demons around the twelfth century. As with any legend, he started small, first appearing in remote villages and mountain towns where the concept of frightening creatures that haunt the highlands was already well understood. The name Krampus is derived from *krampen*, the German word for "claw." It's believed he's the son of Hel, the Norse god of the underworld.

In the thirteenth century, the church tried to eradicate Krampus because he not only looked like their evolving concept of the Devil, but also seemed to glorify and celebrate the dark side of society. I not-so-humbly disagree. Krampus has always been the consequence of bad behavior. One would think the church would welcome the figure, but in an effort to control the narrative, Krampus is frowned upon. Still, the best way to make a pop culture icon even more popular is to ban it. Though Krampus

Gruß vom Krampus

Late 19th-century Krampus postcard, Germany.

emerged in the twelfth century, he wallowed in relative obscurity. It was during the eigteenth and nineteenth century that Krampus came out from the shadows of the mountains and into the limelight of villages and cities.

By the 1800s, Krampus was here to stay in Austria, Bavaria, Slovenia, and the Czech Republic. That doesn't mean Christianity didn't leave its mark on this Yuletide beast. The chains surrounding Krampus are a Christian addition, representing the binding of the Devil. Plus, his features began to reflect more devil-like imagery of the time, like a forked tongue and dramatic horns.

By the second half of the nineteenth century, Krampus was coming into his own. His horrific visage adorned the cover of countless postcards. People mailed them as greeting cards. Artists worked their magic creating horror scenes of Krampus leading children to their holiday doom.

Krampus became a holiday staple in this region of Europe. He began traveling with Saint Nicholas on December 5 and 6 to offer a consequence to the naughty. And he remained a mainstay of the holiday for several decades, right up until two world wars stole the attention of the masses. By the time World War II had ended, when Germany and Austria were dusting themselves off and rebuilding, a new icon had already pushed Krampus into the far corner. Santa Claus was coming to town and gaining global fame not only as the solitary figure related to the Christmas holiday, but also as a tool to help lift a country's economy come December.

So Krampus slunk back to the corners of villages in Austria, where he remained a more obscure tradition. He never vanished. No. He was biding his time. Maybe he knew not just Austria but the world would someday summon him forth once again.

That time arrived in the early 2000s, when a perfect storm of Internet interconnectivity and global turmoil sent the public clicking, browsing,

Krampus vintage postcard, 1876, Austria.

and searching for answers that spoke to something primal. Suddenly, one village's obscure holiday legend spread . . . quickly. Of course, movie deals followed, and now Krampus has gone global. Bigger than he ever was. No longer confined to Austria and Germany, he's in your small town's holiday parades now. Annual Krampus Runs—a parade of Krampuses—are happening all over.

❄ ❄ ❄

The 2015 movie *Krampus*, starring Adam Scott, Toni Collette, and David Koechner, offered a huge, global shot in the arm of the legend that is Krampus. Michael Dougherty (who directed and cowrote the script) reimagined Christmas in the home of the dysfunctional Engel family, where a freak storm shuts everything down, locking the extended family inside as Krampus and other monsters close in. Ultimately, it's Krampus who is coming to save them from ruin by scaring them nearly to death. The film made $61.5 million at the box office off a budget of $15 million. That's a success by Hollywood standards, and the film has since been moving toward cult hit status. Though the movie doesn't follow the lore that closely, I love that they nailed the spirit of what Krampus is. Love the movie or hate it (it scored 66 percent on Rotten Tomatoes), the film launched Krampus to superstardom.

In December 2017, I had the opportunity to attend the Krampus Society of New England's ball in Providence, Rhode Island. We filmed the ball for the "Creepy Christmas" episode of my *New England Legends* television series on PBS. Other than a bunch of Krampuses, I wasn't sure what to expect. The event was held inside the Mediator Stage Hall in Providence. The building is part of the second-oldest Universalist Church in the state. The church bills itself as a space for "free-thinkers and independent spirits." Hosting the Krampus Ball falls into that mission *somewhere*.

I arrived early with my producer partner, Tony Dunne, and photographer Frank Grace. The room was basically a small church with a back section where they set out a buffet. My assumption was that this was a group of cosplayers who made Krampus their Christmas gig, and come spring, they'd go back to whatever other characters suited their fancy. As the Krampuses began to arrive and I got chatty with them, I learned I wasn't totally wrong in my assumption; however, my assessment wasn't fair either. You can't commit to this level of costume detail without caring deeply about what you're creating. It's not just about making a look. For some attendees, it was about *becoming* Krampus.

Richard Sheridan is the head of the three-hundred-member-strong Krampus Society of New England (KSNE). The first year he did a march was 2013. He said:

> Back then, seven or eight of us were dressed as Krampus. We walked
> around Fall River [Massachusetts] a bit, and with traffic driving by,
> a lot of people would slow down, stare, and yell "Krampus!" out the
> window. That's what made me think this thing has potential.

Since 2013, the legend of Krampus has only grown, as has the membership of the KSNE. At the 2017 ball, there were maybe two dozen Krampuses, and even one Saint Nicholas. A woman was offering spankings to raise money for a local charity, and at one point someone brought in their pet goat. Some of the costumes were highly detailed, others less so, but everyone got into the spirit of the evening.

Aretha Kharashqah, from Worcester, Massachusetts, was dressed for the ball with a black, horned mask and a costume with red and black ribbons and strings. "I'm here to do dress-up and celebrate the tradition of Krampus," she said. "Because I'm usually on the naughty list anyway."

Mathew Stacy from Easton, Massachusetts, had large ram horns on top of his head as well as pointed ears and a beaked nose. Covered in fur and a giant chain, his face was painted dark gray to look like something coming out of the wild. "I like old folklorish traditions," he said. "I have no Austrian roots, so there's a kind of cultural appropriation to some degree, but I like a lot of costuming." Three years prior to the 2017 ball, he had an Austrian friend who was trying to start a Krampus tradition among his friends. "So he was the Saint Nick, and I was the Krampus," he said. Now they go around together, including to the Krampus Ball in Providence.

Ernest Sonyi is Stacy's friend. He lives in southern Rhode Island and dressed as Saint Nicholas for the ball. He was the only Saint Nick in attendance. "Saint Nicholas is the star of the show," he said. "I actually grew up with this tradition. My mother grew up in rural Austria, and so we spent a lot of time following the tradition. Krampus and Saint Nicholas came to visit my home every year." I asked him how he felt when he saw this monster enter his home as a child. "It was terrifying," he said and then laughed. He first remembers Krampus and Saint Nicholas visiting when he was about five years old. "Saint Nicholas would come in the house first and read off all the things I did that were good, and also the bad deeds that happened during the year." In short, he was being judged. Krampus never made a move toward young Ernest, but his presence was a constant threat. As frightening as it was, the event was something he looked forward to every year.

Though the 2017 Krampus Ball was my first run-in with the Christmas Devil, it would not be my last.

I first met Adam Wcislek about a decade ago at a paranormal conference in Dundee, Michigan. We share a love of the weird and unexplained.

Adam is based in the Great Black Swamp region of northeast Ohio. He's forty-five years old, an A/V tech by day, a psychic medium by night, and come the holiday season, he's Krampus. In 2019, I gave a talk at the Dundee conference called "Creepy Christmas" (naturally, Krampus was heavily featured). I had arranged it with the organizers ahead of time, explaining Christmas is far more frightening than Halloween. Little did I know, the conference had a surprise for me.

When my talk was finished, I heard a thundering noise from the back of the conference room. A frightening voice told me I'd been bad, a fog machine billowed artificial smoke out of the dressing room at the back, and then out came Krampus! And I mean Krampus! This costume was no joke. The nicest I had ever seen in person. Frightening. Horrible. Bigger than life. In short, it was perfection.

So I reconnected with Adam, the man behind the mask.

He'd never heard about Krampus until around 2012. Back then, Krampus was just one of many strange creatures he found interesting. But in time, he couldn't stop thinking about him. Then the *Krampus* movie came out in 2015. He watched Krampus runs in Austria via YouTube, and soon he was hooked.

"I tried looking around the States," Wcislek said. "Is anybody doing this? Is anybody making this stuff? The more I looked into it, the more I realized it's just not big here."

It wasn't. Not then. But times change quickly. Legends can spread like a virus, especially when there's something both primal and familiar about them.

So Wcislek found an Austrian artist online who carves Krampus masks. He said his handmade mask alone was about $750. He points out that the details of the teeth added to the cost. He commissioned artist

Adam Wcislek with the Krampus mask he commissioned from Stefan Koidl of Hallein, Austria.

Stefan Koidl from Hallein, Austria, who had a one-year waiting list for his hand-carved wooden masks. A look through Koidl's website and Facebook page shows a trove of horror masterpieces.

On the design of the mask, Wcislek said:

> The point was to depict a lot of me, so I wanted the bigger nose, the beard, and the color scheme has to do with how I found Krampus, which was through the paranormal. So, I wanted that kind of ghostly gray look, I wanted cuts in the face, but the eyes, I wanted them to be unique because one of the theories is that it was Saint Nicholas's brother, so I had the eyes done blue. I wanted it to be menacing as an alter-ego of me. But it started here with the mask.

From there, Wcislek had to build the rest of the costume.

> I got pants that have stitching in it, and to make myself more menacing I wear platform boots because I am short. I like a lot of the Renaissance aspects of the clothing. Plus, I have armor underneath all of the fur, so that gives me a little more elevation. I added skulls around my waist too. The only thing I still want to add is an authentic cowbell—like the ones over in Austria. But one of them costs 200 bucks.

He figures he's about $1,600 to $1,800 in on this costume right now. What's he doing with all of this? He went to a local "Meet Kris Kringle" event last year, and then he came out as Krampus, to the surprise of all. "I'd love to be able to get out more and spread the word about Krampus."

It takes him between twenty-five and forty-five minutes to don the costume. It takes time to position the fur and get his legs roped off to cover the boots, and he needs helpers to accomplish the task of becoming

Krampus. He doesn't currently do any other kind of cosplay; he just loves Krampus and how he feels behind the mask.

It's easy for me to see how big Krampus is getting in the United States. Plus, my usual social circles tend to intersect with people interested in strange monsters who eat children. Add in the horror element, the cosplay, and what's not to love? But I also wanted the Austrian perspective, so I reached out to the Krampus museum located in Ruatn-Pass, Kitzbühel, Austria. I had the opportunity to interview the museum's founder, Christoph Rieser, with the help of his sister, Katharina, who speaks more English than her brother.

Rieser is thirty-two years old and is one of a small group of people who earns his entire living off Krampus. He not only runs the museum, but also makes most of his living carving Krampus masks and making the full costumes for customers all over the world. He was introduced to Krampus at age six when his parents brought him to his first Krampus festival.

He explained that back then, Krampus only came out on December 5. Each village had a few people who would dress up and walk down the street on *Krampusnacht*—Krampus night. They didn't receive much media attention; it was simply a tradition that survived. But times have changed. Today, the Krampus runs start in early November and continue through December 6.

The museum looks like half Halloween horror fun house and half museum of masks. Rooms are dramatically lit or made to look like a forest with Krampus monsters appearing like they're ready to leap out and grab you. As of this writing, there are 970 masks in the collection, taking up over ten thousand square feet of space, with the oldest Krampus mask dating back to 1903.

Rieser said that he founded the museum in 2008 after the mayor asked him to carve a custom mask. Rieser's father explained that his son would need space to work on the mask, so the mayor gave him the key to the building that houses the current museum. Located below the spectator stand of the Court Küchenmeister, near the Sportpark in Kitzbühel, the space had been one giant, empty room for almost thirty years. "It was completely full of junk," he said.

With some help from his friends, they emptied the space and built a room in which to work, as well as a room to house the masks. Each year they hold a Krampus festival in Kitzbühel where they sell food and other items that help fund the museum. As years passed, its reputation and collection grew. Rooms and masks were added as time and money allowed. Today, interest in the museum and collection is only increasing as Krampus's international reputation grows.

Rieser makes about thirty Krampus masks per year. The price for a custom mask is anywhere from $500 to $600 for the basic mask, and up to $1,200 depending on the horns and level of detail.

The masks are made from Swiss stone pine. It's light, it's native to the region, and it smells nice. It takes Rieser forty to forty-five hours to make the mask, from cutting the wood with a chainsaw, to hand-carving and painting. He also makes the fur costume and sells the bells that adorn the final costume. He said many of his customers are located in the United States.

I asked him why he believes Krampus is getting so popular worldwide now. He said:

> Because people who dress like Krampus and become Krampus, they get to act out the darker side of their personality. Also, when you wear the mask, you can be someone else. They don't trust themselves to act this way without the mask. You can be

another person. You can switch into another role and become the Krampus.

In modern Krampus runs, Krampus often carries a tree branch or a switch of sticks. He may even strike your feet with the sticks if you're watching the parade.

According to Rieser:

It's not to hurt you. It's to hit the bad ghosts—to drive them out of you so you'll be safe this coming winter. It's also why Krampus wears the bells. Not for the living people, but to ward off the bad winter ghosts.

So, sure, lately Krampus has become more of a good guy under a scary façade, but that doesn't mean the old threats aren't still relevant. Rieser is the father of a young girl. He said, "I tell her when she doesn't do as she's told, that the Krampus will come pick you up and take you back to his house!"

After children walk through the Krampus museum and see the wonderfully horrific sights and hundreds of masks, each of them featured in some Krampus parade, the threat of abduction must chill the deepest parts of their psyche . . . which was always the point of Krampus.

Though the legend of Krampus has evolved to where he might hit you with sticks to drive out the bad winter ghosts, traditionally speaking, he was there to administer punishment on behalf of Saint Nicholas. And sometimes, if warranted, that punishment turned deadly.

8

Belsnickel

rampus may be too lethal for your liking. I understand. It's frightening to think of monsters hunting for our naughty children, because the optimist in us believes that even the worst children can be redeemed if given the right chances and . . . *motivation*. Fortunately, there's a Yuletide figure who can offer that motivation in the form of a brutal beating. Enter the Belsnickel.

Belsnickel hails from the Palatinate region in Europe, which lies in the central-southwestern part of Germany. His bearded face is streaked with soot, and his clothes are a tattered patchwork of furs. Sometimes he may wear antlers fastened to his head to give himself a monstrous, half-animal look. In his hand, he carries a switch of sticks. His name translates to "Nicholas in Furs." He travels alone.

He's here to pass judgment . . . and a beating.

The Belsnickel shows up at your home one to two weeks before Christmas as a welcome sight for parents, but not so much for children—for the kids, the Belsnickel is there to inquire, test, and pass judgment. He carries with him rewards like candies and cakes, but that switch is *not* just for show.

After being welcomed into a home by parents, he'll gather the children in one room. Maybe he'll place some sweets and cakes on the table—but don't go grabbing for them without asking! The sweets are part of the test. Kids who grab are soon smacked with the sticks. Just a warning at first, but keep testing the Belsnickel and you'll pay the price.

Yet for some children there's no escaping the wrath of the Belsnickel. Parents simply point out the naughtiest kids upon the Belsnickel's arrival. The Belsnickel nods and knows what to do next. That wicked child will be

Belsnickel and naughty child, late 19th-century postcard.

Saint Nicholas and his companion Knecht Ruprecht knocking on the window,
illustration, late 19th century, Germany.

taken outside, tied to a tree, and beaten. The hope is that this punishment will be enough to get the naughty child back on the right path so they're worthy of presents for Christmas.

The Belsnickel has been around since the seventeenth century. Many believe he's a derivative of a cousin in northern Germany called Knecht Ruprecht. *Knecht Ruprecht* translates to "farmhand" or "servant Rupert" (or "Robert"), a companion of Saint Nicholas who first showed up in the city of Nuremberg. Knecht Ruprecht accompanies Saint Nicholas to punish the naughty children while Nicholas rewards the good ones. Ruprecht is literally a servant of Saint Nicholas, and like a servant, he does the dirty work so his master can keep his hands clean. The roles of these cohorts may sound familiar to that of Krampus, which is logical considering all of these creatures hail from roughly the same region of Europe.

Ruprecht's dress is basic and matches that of any peasant farmhand. He carries a bag of ashes (which explains his soot-covered face). As his legend spread throughout Germany, the Belsnickel was born. The distance from Nuremberg to the Palatinate region is only 150 miles—which is not very far for a legend to travel and evolve as a new region adds its own touches, to the point where it becomes something new entirely. The biggest difference between Knecht Ruprecht and Belsnickel is that Belsnickel doesn't need Saint Nicholas by his side to do his work.

I first met the Belsnickel in December of 2015. We were searching for a holiday-themed story for my *New England Legends* series, and we heard about a historic home called the Smith-Harris House (now called the Brookside Farm Museum) in Niantic, Connecticut, that brought in the Belsnickel for the children at Christmas. At the time, I had never heard of the Belsnickel, but after a little research, I knew we had to grab our cameras and head down there.

The home was built in 1845 by Thomas Avery. It's been preserved as a museum since 1976. Stepping inside was like walking back in time, with fireplaces in several rooms, antique furniture, and décor appropriate to the nineteenth century. Already decked out for the holiday, they had Christmas trees in multiple rooms adorned with old-fashioned ornaments. Currier and Ives would be pleased with the whole look.

That's when Gary Lakowsky walked into the room. Short in stature, bespectacled, with a neatly trimmed gray beard, he'd been volunteering at the museum for years. But once he streaked his face with soot, picked up a stick, and donned the furs—cut from a former fur coat that had been out of fashion to wear for any other purpose for decades—Gary transformed into the Belsnickel.

The museum's director, Joanie DiMartino, had arranged for some children to attend for the purposes of our filming. I had pulled Joanie aside and asked how authentic their Belsnickel was. She said, "What do you mean?" I followed up asking if he was going to beat any of these young kids. She said their Belsnickel doesn't do that. Which I understand is stating the obvious, because beating children at Christmas is the kind of thing that makes national news.

Five young kids gathered in front of the fireplace to experience the Belsnickel. The youngest was maybe two, and the oldest was twelve or thirteen. A fire burned, adding the perfect ambiance. When the Belsnickel entered the room, the kids turned to see him and smiled. He had some candy to offer and told the kids the story of the Belsnickel—mostly for the benefit of our cameras. Still, I know a thing or two about star power. I've seen young kids nearly faint when Santa walks into the room. The Belsnickel hasn't reached that level yet. Or maybe I should say he hasn't *returned* to that level of fame yet. There was a time in small villages in Germany where his presence would have been a much bigger deal. Still, the fact that he's become an annual tradition at a historic museum in Connecticut is a sign he's coming back.

When Germans immigrated to the United States, they brought the Belsnickel with them. In eastern Pennsylvania, where large populations of Germans settled, the Belsnickel never went away. And if his appearance in a small coastal Connecticut town isn't enough to convince you of his imminent return, we need only to turn to mass media.

On December 6, 2012, season nine of NBC's hit show *The Office* (which is set in the eastern Pennsylvania town of Scranton) featured an episode called "Dwight Christmas," in which the character Dwight Schrute shows up to the office party dressed as the Belsnickel, complete with a soot-covered face, clothed in furs, and ready to dole out punishment to his officemates. Dwight explains, "I was born to be Belsnickel." To which his coworker Jim replies, "So he's kind of like Santa. Except dirty. And worse."

In 2020, Netflix released the holiday movie *The Christmas Chronicles: Part Two* starring Kurt Russell as Santa Claus and Goldie Hawn as Mrs. Claus. The story follows a teenage girl named Kate who, upset about her mother's new relationship, runs off to the North Pole, where she unknowingly assists a naughty entity named Belsnickel in trying to cancel Christmas.

In the movie, the Belsnickel is played by Julian Dennison, who is covered neither in furs nor soot. However, the teen wears a black jacket, so we know he's a bad guy. In reality, the Belsnickel is no enemy of Santa Claus—but still, a few more mainstream appearances like these and the Belsnickel may just show up in your next holiday parade. And then who knows? Maybe there'll be a knock at your door a few weeks before Christmas.

The best part of the traditional Belsnickel is that people in your village may take turns being the Belsnickel each year. So this Christmas you may get to travel door-to-door and beat my children, and next Christmas, maybe it's my turn to beat yours.

9

A Knock at the Door

nd if you're going door to door . . . well you might as well go under the guise of goodness and song. Right? I mean there's nothing creepy about a bunch of strangers gathering at your door. Or a bunch of your neighbors in masks. In the dark. In the cold. Singing. Demanding libations and presents.

Today we call it "caroling," but that's a modern misnomer. And as with everything related to this festive holiday, its roots run deep.

Here we come a-wassailing
Among the leaves so green;
Here we come a-wand'ring
So fair to be seen.

Love and joy come to you,
And to you your wassail too;
And God bless you and send you a Happy New Year
And God send you a Happy New Year.

Our wassail cup is made
Of the rosemary tree,
And so is your beer
Of the best barley.

"Wassailing" was a term I was familiar with thanks to this classic holiday song. For years, I thought the term was interchangeable with "caroling," thanks to hearing this same exact song with the variation "Here we come a-caroling." But that's not quite right.

There was a time in the Celtic region of the world when Pagan groups would gather in orchards and sing songs to the fruit trees to appease the spirits of the orchard. In addition to singing, the wassailers would bang on metal and make a ruckus to scare off bad spirits. The intent was to ask for a bountiful harvest the following year. The grateful owner of the orchard was expected to reward the singers with a warm, spiced, boozy beverage in a big bowl that would be shared among the group. The drink could be a warmed ale or beer with mulled spices, or a cider of some kind. Nothing *too* strong, or else the singers may get belligerent. Just strong enough to keep them toasty and happy.

We sing to scare away bad spirits.

Sometimes farmers would ask for this same ritual of singing and scaring away bad spirits to be performed on their animals. The payment was the same, though: treats, booze, and sometimes money.

The Celtic reign ended as the Roman Empire spread into their homelands in western Europe during the first century CE, but that doesn't mean the Celtic ways were completely lost. They just changed labels. People still sang and drank at harvest time. It just moved indoors over the centuries.

Though the exact origin of the term "wassailing" is unknown, it appears to be a derivative of the Anglo-Saxon greeting *waes hail*, which translates to "be in good health." It was a common toast offered by the most esteemed guest in attendance. The guest would lift the bowl of punch, proclaim *waes hail*, and then pass the bowl. The person next to the initial toaster would offer a response, and the toast and bowl moved around the room, each person drinking from the communal pot, signifying they were all equals that night.

During the 1600s, wassailing moved back outdoors and became associated with Twelfth Night activities. The Twelfth Night is January 5—

twelve days after Christmas. People fasted for Advent between December 1 and 24, so Christmas Day started twelve days of partying that culminated with drunken revelry on Twelfth Night.

> *Call up the butler of this house,*
> *Put on his golden ring.*
> *Let him bring us up a glass of beer,*
> *And better we shall sing.*

Wassailers would carry their large wassailing bowl, often made from wood, to the homes of their wealthy neighbors, sing their songs, and hopefully get their bowl filled with more booze. They may also ask for money.

> *We have got a little purse*
> *Of stretching leather skin;*
> *We want a little of your money*
> *To line it well within.*

Ultimately, the wassailers offered their blessing if they were pleased with their payment.

> *God bless the master of this house*
> *Likewise the mistress too,*
> *And all the little children*
> *That round the table go.*

Finally, the wassailers parted with a message that those inside were better off than those outside—that they should count their blessings.

> *Good master and good mistress,*
> *While you're sitting by the fire,*
> *Pray think of us poor children*
> *Who are wandering in the mire.*

"The Wassail Bowl at Christmas," English illustration, 1860.

All in good fun, right? Sure. But by the 1700s, though the celebration of Christmas was not really a *thing* like we know it today, the wassailing tradition came roaring back, and with less civility than before. The singers were still drunk, but now they were angry. The songs were less *request* and more *demand* for libations, food, and money.

So what changed? The Industrial Revolution, for one.

By the latter half of the eighteenth century, factories were popping up all over Europe, with the American colonies following soon after. Factories offered low pay and grueling hours. Running water from streams, rivers, and man-made lakes and pond runoffs drove enormous waterwheels that powered machines in these factories. Now the world could produce goods quickly and cheaply. We were entering a brave new world full of automation. These factories made some people very rich, while their employees struggled to get by. The gap between the haves and have-nots grew into a wide canyon.

By December, factory owners in northern regions had two big problems. First, there was less daylight, so workers couldn't work as many hours. Second, at some point, ponds, lakes, and even rivers froze, meaning the factories shut down, and workers were left laid off until the spring.

With idle time, and desperate finances, these poor workers took the opportunity to resurrect some old Yule-time ways.

Wassailing now looked more like a drunken mob bordering on a dangerous riot, as the rabble hammered their fists on doors of the well-to-do employers, demanding good food and drink. The wealthy now had a decision to make. They could get rough with their out-of-work employees and their families. They could send out the brute squad to rough 'em up and move them along. Or they could play along.

In short, Christmas was turning back into something it had been ever since they called it Saturnalia—an annual steam valve. A time for the common people to tie one on, party with the rich, get a handout or two, and settle in to survive the long, dull winter.

Mummering

Mummers are wassailers who've been thrown on the Island of Misfit Toys.

Mummering was born in England, where troupes of actors would act out plays. One popular play was the Middle Ages story of Saint George and the Dragon. The plot involves George, who arrives in a small village where the locals have been terrorized by a dragon. Before George's arrival, the villagers were forced to sacrifice a sheep each day to feed the scaly monster. But when the village ran out of sheep, the king proclaimed they must sacrifice a child each day to keep the dragon from running amok.

The children were chosen by lottery, until one day the king's daughter was picked. Thankfully for the king, that was the day George was passing through the village. George was astonished at what was happening, so he offered to kill the dragon. George stalked the beast to discover a vulnerable patch under the dragon's arm, where he successfully slayed the beast.

Saint George would go on to become the patron saint of England. And to give credit where it's due, I can confirm that there are *no* dragons in England anymore. I've been there multiple times and checked.

Mummers act out this play dressed in crude disguises—disguises like a sheet over one's face with eye and mouth holes cut out. Underwear may be worn outside of one's clothes. Basically, if you spent more than five

minutes and five bucks on your mummering costume, you did something wrong. Men dress as women, women dress as men, and masks are worn. The point is to disguise yourself, because you're visiting your neighbors who know everyone in the village, so they must guess at who you might be. Mummers also disguise their voices.

Mummering is not a big deal in England anymore, yet it survives and even thrives in St. John's, Newfoundland, Canada. The earliest record of mummering in Newfoundland dates back to 1819. Given the region's predominantly British and Irish population, it makes sense that these groups brought mummering over from their homeland. In the mid-nineteenth century, mummering was popular there around Christmastime. But then something terrible happened. In December of 1860, in the town of Bay Roberts, a local fisherman named Isaac Mercer was walking home when a group of six mummers jumped him and beat him to a pulp. They picked him up and walked him home, but Mercer died in his sleep that night.

Mercer was a Protestant. His attackers were Catholic. This was during a time when these two groups were *not* getting along in Newfoundland. Mummering had always been unruly, but now the practice had turned lethal. So the government stepped in. On June 25, 1861, the Act to Make Further Provision for the Prevention of Nuisances was passed. *Great name, right?* Anyway, the law was clear: "Any Person who shall be found, at any Season of the Year . . . without a written License from a Magistrate, dressed as a Mummer, masked, or otherwise disguised, shall be deemed guilty of a Public Nuisance." Basically, you needed a permit to go mummering.

However, the following year an amendment to that act was passed, making mummering illegal in Newfoundland, period. And illegal it remained until 1992 when the act was repealed.

Just because it was illegal doesn't mean it wasn't practiced in pockets and villages. In the nineteenth century, mummering in Newfoundland was

The Philadelphia Mummers Parade. "A procession of masquerades passing the Post-Office,"
December 1892.

dangerous. Back then they called it Mummers and Fools. Some mummers would procure a pig's bladder from a butcher, fill it with rocks, and hit people with it as they marched in their mini parades. Combine the 1861 murder with the violence, and it's easy to see why the government would want to put a stop to mummering. In short, the fool-to-mummer ratio was leaning too heavily toward the fools.

But then mummering returned in a big way to Newfoundland on the back of a 1983 folk tune called "The Mummer's Song," by a duo from Fortune Bay called Simani. The song features an accordion and an almost polka beat. The first verse goes:

> Don't seem like Christmas if the Mummers are not here,
> Granny would say as she'd knit in her chair;
> Things have gone modern and I s'pose
> that's the cause,
> Christmas is not like it was.

If you think about it, Christmas has never been like it was. It's been evolving and changing for millennia. That's what it does. Still, this song was a regional hit. It got Newfies thinking how fun that tradition was, and how they could go door-to-door drinking in a big-raging-party kind of way once again. And just like that, some folks in St. John's donned some silly clothes and crude masks, warned their livers of what was about to go down when copious booze arrived, and headed out on December 26. Boxing Day. The Second Day of Christmas.

One of those mummers who caught the revival feeling is my friend Raylene Ball. Now fifty-one, she's a born-and-raised St. John's Newfie. She's a seventh- and eighth-grade history teacher who held up her history book to show me that mummering is part of their curriculum! Yet Ball has her own fond memories of the activity.

"Mummering in Newfoundland is mostly an adult thing," Ball said. "When I grew up in town, there really wasn't much mummering anyway. It was more around the rural parts."

"Around the Bay" is how the locals refer to the rural parts of town where mummering was more popular. Which makes sense. If a group of masked strangers comes knocking at your door in a city, you're taking your chances of getting robbed, killed, both, or worse. Plus, remember Isaac Mercer?

Mummers make a ruckus . . . or worse.

Ball explained how mummering used to take place anytime between December 26 and January 6. But when it made its revival in the 1980s, some people started doing it just before Christmas—their own version of caroling.

Ball recalls that back in the 1980s, some mummer troops would reenact the St. George and the Dragon play as part of their tradition, taking mummering back to its English roots.

There's one other factor that boosted mummering back into the Newfoundland mainstream. It's no coincidence that it happened in 1992, the same year that the act making mummering illegal was repealed. In 1992, cod fishing was banned in Newfoundland.

"My great-grandfather was a schooner captain, and my grandfather was a cod fisherman. This ban completely changed Newfoundland," Ball said. "In one day, 32,000 people were thrown out of work on an island with a total population of 250,000 people."

The economy was crippled. People were poor, out of work. And mummering came roaring back in Newfoundland.

"This is when mummering really took off, because that's the time I did it," Ball said. "Into the nineties it just became bigger and bigger."

When you're mummering, the point is to entertain the homeowners. Ball explains, "You bang on the door, you disguise your voice, and you say, 'Any mummers 'llowed in?' They invite you in, and you go rogue and take over their house. You sing, you dance a jig, while people try to guess who you are. You can't just stand there."

Mummers may also carry instruments like an accordion, a guitar, a fiddle, or an *ugly stick*. The ugly stick is a stick with beer caps and washers nailed into it. The bottom is a rubber boot, and some people might put a wig on top. You take a second stick and beat the first so it makes a jingling sound. Mummers may spend ten to fifteen minutes at a house before moving on to the next one. Making a ruckus. Delivering good cheer. Driving out the bad.

"It's mostly a party," Ball said. An excuse to drink. "The details at the beginning of the night are very clear. The details toward five o'clock in the morning are a little sketchy."

In Pennsylvania, Philadelphians have been mummering en masse since 1901. The parade has been happening each year ever since and has grown to epic proportions, making it the longest-running mummers' parade in the United States. Today more than ten thousand rowdy revelers gather in Philly on January 2 to sing, dance, and party their way around City Hall.

The only way some of us can truly be ourselves is to hide behind a mask and imbibe libations. For others, the disguises allow the monsters within to come out.

10

Mari Lwyd

here's a famous painting hanging in the National Gallery in Oslo, Norway, by Peter Nicolai Arbo called *Åsgårdsreien*. The translation is "Ride of Asgard." Asgard is the land of the gods, and Odin is its King. This painting depicts Odin's wild and noisy ride. When autumn's leaves die and fall, and Midwinter approaches, Odin's wagon and horses ride through the sky on a hunt, accompanied by his ravens and wolves as they chase down the souls of the dead. You know when the hunt is on because you can hear the roar outside. You may think it's the winter wind whipping through the bare trees, but maybe it's really the Wild Hunt. If you're going to participate, you'll need a horse.

The hunt is on.

In southern Wales, a Midwinter monster rises from the grave sometime between Christmas Day and Twelfth Night in search of libations and treats. The Mari Lwyd (pronounced *mah-di load*) is a pale horse that can cross from the underworld into our world. The Welsh translation is "the Gray Mare." She's covered in a white sheet. Her head is a horse's skull adorned with ribbons for a mane. She may have bulbs for eyes, bells jingle from her bridle, and she may be covered in electric lights in our modern times. As for those human legs sticking out below the sheet— try to ignore them.

The Mari Lwyd is led by an *ostler*, a person who traditionally looks after the horses of guests staying at an inn. There are likely other people accompanying the mare and handler as they go wassailing throughout the village. When they arrive at a home, they sing Welsh songs as

Åsgårdsreien by Peter Nicolai Arbo, 1872. National Gallery of Norway.

they engage in *pwnco*, where the wassailers participate in a rhyming verse exchange with the occupants of the house. Often these rhymes are rude and crude. Sometimes they're improvised, other times they're traditional rhymes. The objective is for the Mari Lwyd and her handlers to come up with a superior verse so that the homeowner relents and allows the Gray Mare and her group inside. If the Mari Lwyd gains entry, it's said to bring good luck to the household for the coming year. However, there's a downside. The Mari Lwyd and her crew are mischievous, they've likely been drinking (and expect the homeowner to provide more), and they may try to steal items or pull other pranks. Mari may impishly chase people as she makes her way through the house and village.

Celtic and British lore has various traditions related to pale horses who could cross from our world into the next and back again. There's the Gallic Epona, the Irish Macha, and the Welsh Rhiannon—a horse goddess. The Mari Lwyd is likely derived from those earlier legends blended with Odin's Wild Hunt, combining it with wassailing, where the poor entertain locals with song and dance in exchange for money and food handouts during the harsh winter months.

The first time the Mari Lwyd appears in print is in the Reverend J. Evans's 1800 book, *A Tour through North Wales*. Evans writes:

Another very singular custom, I never could learn the *rationale* of is, that of a man on new year's day, dressing himself in blankets and other trappings, with a factitious head like a horse, and a party attending him, knocking for admittance, this obtained, he runs about the room with an uncommon frightful noise, which the company quit in real or pretended fright; they soon recover, and by reciting a verse of some ancient *cowydd* [a traditional form of

A contemporary Christmas card © Kim Thompson. Used by permission.

rhyming Welsh poetry], or in default, paying a small gratuity, they gain admission.

It doesn't *have* to be rational, Rev. J. Sometimes we do things because they're fun, or just to stir the pot.

The Mari Lwyd likely existed long before Rev. Evans wrote about her in 1800. But once the Mari Lwyd made it into print, then it was just a matter of time. In my experience, when an activity leads to free booze and sweets, it's going to spread. While mostly in good fun, not everyone was a fan of Mari. One Baptist minister called Mari "sinful" in his 1852 book. And if not sinful, other clergy saw too many Pagan roots in Mari Lwyd for their liking. However, any publicity is good publicity. If clergy calls something "sinful," others will want to inquire as to what the fuss is about, and the legend grows.

By the 1930s and '40s, the Mari Lwyd tradition was all but dying out. Still, she survived in pockets of the country. Southern Welsh cities like Cardiff, Bridgend, Llangynwyd, Neath, and Glamorgan still saw the Mari Lwyd trotting around Christmastime. The 1960s and '70s saw perhaps the lowest point in Mari popularity, with only a few small groups keeping the tradition alive.

However, the Internet age has brought Mari Lwyd back with a vengeance. There are Facebook groups dedicated to building your own hobby-horse Mari Lwyd, self-help videos explaining how to take the horse's skull and configure just the right snap to the jaw, and annual festivals reviving a wild ride through Midwinter legend and lore as the rabble spread a little mischief and misrule.

II

Grýla

here's no question that Krampus steals the headlines. He's got that look, you know? But now he's gone Hollywood. He eats at restaurants we couldn't even walk by because they're so exclusive. Yet he's not the only monster we need to fear this holiday season. For even darker holiday horror, we need to travel to Iceland to meet the frigid Queen of Christmas. A witch; an ogress who lives in a cave in the hinterlands of Iceland.

In Iceland, Midwinter is known as *jól* (or Yule). It's dark. The sun barely rises this far north. It's cold. And now we have to watch out for a beastly troll of a woman who hunts children. The first time Grýla appears in writing dates back to the thirteenth century, when some of the great historic Icelandic sagas and poems were first documented.

> *Down comes Grýla from the outer fields*
> *With forty tails*
> *A bag on her back, a sword/knife in her hand,*
> *Coming to carve out the stomachs of the children*
> *Who cry for meat during Lent.*

Grýla loosely translates to "Growler" in English. In those early days, she wasn't specifically associated with Midwinter and instead represented more of a constant threat that lived in the mountains but came down to hunt. Parents were more than happy to share her story with their children too. The more horrific the telling, the better, because if you could keep your children afraid of the mountains—particularly in the long and dark winter nights—you kept them safer. As a parent, you had to figure that even if the Grýla didn't abduct and kill your children in those woods, there were plenty of other dangers that might do the killing on behalf of the mountain ogress. Over time, though, she tied one of her many tails to *jól* and has remained there ever since.

A large and beastly ogress, the Grýla is feared by all. There's a story of her eating one of her husbands because she was bored with him. Then there are the children who live in constant fear of ending up as an ingredient in one of her stews.

The "Growler" is a large and beastly ogress.

For help with all things Icelandic and monstrous, I connected with Terry Gunnell, professor of Folkloristics at the University of Iceland. Gunnell was born in England, but Iceland has been his home since 1979. Based in Reykjavík, Gunnell is also an author and expert on Icelandic legend and lore. We talked about Grýla as well as her dysfunctional family, the Yule Lads, and the Yule Cat. More on them next.

"All of these figures are associated with the wild," Gunnell explained. To put it into context, he said when Iceland was first settled around 900 CE, it was all open. There were no humans there yet. But soon after Europeans first arrived, people built farms and then towns. They would clear the land to make an area for themselves. They changed the landscape. The spirits were then forced to move farther out, or up into the mountains. He said the farthest area out in the wild is the realm of trolls, the outlaws. And closer to the farms are the hidden people, the elves, the nature spirits, and the fairies.

In the early nineteenth century, Grýla began her association with Midwinter. During this time of year in Iceland, it's customary to bring together your relatives—both the living and the dead—to celebrate the season and to prepare for the long winter ahead. In attendance at the festivities were not only the living and the ghosts, but the elves and the trolls, whether they were invited or not. To the delight of some, and the deepest fright of others, sometimes these magical trolls and elves would visit in the flesh during these holiday parties, often as friends and relatives dressed in costumes and masks, helping to turn the legend into reality for the children.

The spirit world isn't so abstract in Iceland, even today. Gunnell told me that his wife blesses their home on New Year's Eve with a lit candle while offering an Icelandic phrase: *"Koma þeir sem koma vilja. Veri þeir sem vera vilja. Fara þeir sem fara vilja. Mér og mínum að meinalausu."* This means "Come all those who wish to come, stay all those who wish to stay, leave all those who wish to leave, but bring no harm to me or my family," Gunnell said.

Today, there are Grýla decorations throughout Iceland during the holiday season. At the Keflavík Airport outside of Reykjavík, there's a display of a hag-like Grýla sitting over a large cauldron, making her stew. Visitors can sit in the giant pot and pose for pictures. Similar displays can be found around the country.

As Grýla became intertwined with the Christmas holiday during the Christianization of Iceland, other Icelandic creatures joined this highly dysfunctional and deadly family of monsters. Enter the Yule Lads.

12

Yule Lads

ýla is not alone as she terrorizes Icelanders and their children. She has thirteen children who each show up on specific days in December and then stay for two weeks. Their presence compounds as each day another Yule Lad arrives, until day thirteen when all of them appear at once. Each Yule Lad offers his own form of torment. We'll take them in turn.

1. **Stekkjarstaur,** *Sheep-Cote Clod,* December 12 to December 25. Stekkjarstaur harasses your sheep. However, with two peg legs, he's not the most mobile.

2. **Giljagaur,** *Gully Gawk,* December 13 to December 26. Giljagaur lurks hidden near your barn, waiting for the opportunity to sneak inside and steal your cow's milk.

3. **Stúfur,** *Stubby,* December 14 to December 27. This Lad is unusually short and lurks around your kitchen to swipe your pans and eat any crust you may have left behind.

4. **Þvörusleikir,** *Spoon-Licker,* December 15 to December 28. Þvörusleikir also lurks in your kitchen to steal and lick wooden spoons you've used in your cooking. This poor Lad appears thin and malnourished.

5. **Pottaskefill,** *Pot-Scraper,* December 16 to December 29. If your kitchen pots are unattended after your meals, Pottaskefill will steal your leftovers.

6. **Askasleikir,** *Bowl-Licker,* December 17 to December 30. If you bring a bowl of gruel or warm cereal to eat in bed before you drift off to sleep, this Lad is waiting under your bed for when you set the bowl on the floor. That's when he slides the bowl underneath and licks it clean.

7. **Hurðaskellir,** *Door-Slammer,* December 18 to December 31. Well named, Hurðaskellir will slam your doors in the middle of the night! You'll get little rest this holiday season when you're startled awake by this menace of a Yule Lad.

8. **Skyrgámur,** *Skyr-Gobbler,* December 19 to January 1. Skyr is a thick, Icelandic yogurt. If you have any on hand this holiday season, Skyrgámur will steal it.

9. **Bjúgnakrækir,** *Sausage-Swiper,* December 20 to January 2. This Lad hides in your rafters near where you're smoking your sausage and swipes them when you're not looking.

10. **Gluggagægir,** *Window-Peeper,* December 21 to January 3. Did you see someone peeking in your window? A peeping Tom, or a pesky Yule Lad? If it's near Christmas, it may be Gluggagægir.

11. **Gáttaþefur,** *Doorway-Sniffer,* December 22 to January 4. This oversized-nosed Lad has a sniffer that's acutely attuned to laufabrauð, or leaf bread, a holiday favorite crisp flatbread with intricate patterns. Get yours while you can before the Doorway-Sniffer grabs them all.

12. **Ketkrókur,** *Meat-Hook,* December 23 to January 5. Ketkrókur uses a hook to steal your meat right off the table, the kitchen counter, or the fridge. Your dinner isn't safe for these two weeks.

13. **Kertasníkir,** *Candle-Stealer,* December 24 to January 6. There was a time when candles were made from tallow, or animal fat. They were edible, which is unfortunate because Kertasníkir has a taste for them. This Lad will follow children to swipe their candles around Christmas.

"All Icelandic families, especially those with children, are very aware of the Christmas Lads," said Professor Gunnell. "As we get into Christmas, they'll be on the news. For example, who's coming next." Gunnell mentioned that today, kids will take school trips or go with their families to the National Museum in Reykjavík, where they sing songs with people dressed as the Yule Lads and take pictures with the characters.

Each Yule Lad offers his own form of torment.

While all these Yule Lads sound like benevolent fun today, they used to be more sinister. The more traditional Yule Lads would make their way down from the mountains in December and slip into the villages and homes of people, if only for a few weeks. "They came back down as landlords," Gunnell said, "demanding their annual sacrifice. Their annual rent." The Lads came to take, not give.

Over time, their legend and reputation softened to the point where children would place a shoe on their windowsills beginning on December 12, when Stekkjarstaur showed up first. If the children had been good, candy or a treat was left in their shoe. If the children had been naughty, they got a potato. Over the past century, the Yule Lads have transformed into gift-givers instead of rent-takers. They even started to dress more like Santa's helpers, with red and white costumes looking more like Coca-Cola elves than Yule Lads. But over the past twenty years, Gunnell says there's been a slow return to more traditional Yule Lads. Whether that means their behavior may also return to the old ways remains to be seen. I plan to hide my skyr and sausage just in case. I also plan to wear some new clothes, because I still need to contend with the Yule Cat.

13
The Yule Cat

ólakötturinn, or the Yule Cat, as he's known in English, accompanies Grýla and the Yule Lads each holiday season. The Yule Cat is Grýla's lethal pet. A witch's familiar, if you will, though that's putting my Western view of the world on a region that doesn't have witches with cats. The only way to avoid the wrath of the Yule Cat is to wear new clothes at Christmas.

"The Yule Cat is a monster that comes down from the mountains with this rather dysfunctional family," said Professor Terry Gunnell. While that may sound odd, like everything else surrounding this holiday, it's steeped in tradition, or at least adapted from other traditions.

In Scandinavia, you have the Christmas Goat. "Goat" in Swedish is *get*. There were no goats in Iceland, and *get* sounded close-ish to the Icelandic word for cat, so Scandinavia's Yule Goat became Iceland's Yule Cat. Gunnell explained, "If you don't have new clothes, you either become or you [get consumed by] the Christmas Goat or the Christmas Cat. In Iceland, everybody has to wear something new at Christmas so you don't get eaten by the cat."

You must wear new clothes—or else get eaten.

There was a time when farmers encouraged their workers to process all of the autumn wool before Christmas. The farmers would promise their workers new clothes if they could meet the deadline. And to offer further incentive, the farmers told their workers that if they didn't get the wool processed in time, they wouldn't get new clothes, and the Yule Cat would hunt them down, kill them, and eat them.

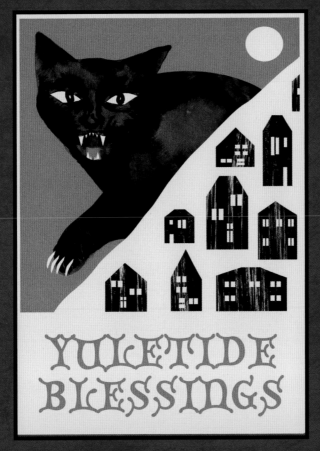

The Yule Cat looms large and menacing. A contemporary Christmas card © Kim Thompson. Used by permission.

The Yule Cat is slinking his way into modern pop culture. Like the Belsnickel, he also made an appearance in the 2020 Netflix movie *The Christmas Chronicles: Part Two*. The Yule Cat accompanies Belsnickel in his quest to ruin Christmas.

Today in Iceland, the Yule Cat does help drive the Christmas economy a little bit. If everyone has to buy some new clothes in December, that's going to boost spending and retail profits. Centuries ago, this was still true, though to a lesser extent, as most people made their own clothes but still had to buy the materials. Though the Yule Cat isn't depicted as lethal as he once was, considering the recent trend of returning to older ways, perhaps this kitten will bare his claws once again.

14

Tomten

n the Scandinavian region of the world—in and around Denmark, Norway, and Sweden—you need all the help you can get managing your farm or home. Harsh climates have a way of compounding life's challenges. Thankfully, you have help in the form of Nordic gnomes called the Tomten.

A Tomte—the singular form of Tomten—is a little elf-like creature. He's all beard and hat, with tiny feet poking out from beneath the bottom of his body-length white beard. He's here to help, sure, but he's also here to keep you in line. He'll look after the animals and make sure you're tending to your own household chores, but if he catches you slacking, he's been known to slap you around as a way to get you back on track. In short, this gnome monitors your behavior.

This gnome will keep you in line.

In 1881, one of Sweden's best-loved poets, Viktor Rydberg, penned "Midvinternattens köld är hård," better known as "Tomten." "Midvinternattens köld är hård" refers to the first line of the poem. *The 1917 Anthology of Swedish Lyrics* offers a translation of Rydberg's "The House Goblin: Tomten."

> *Cold is the night, and still, and strange,*
> *Stars they glitter and shimmer.*
> *All are asleep in the lonely grange*
> *Under the midnight's glimmer.*
> *On glides the moon in gulfs profound;*
> *Snow on the firs and pines around,*

Christmas card, 1899, by Jenny Nyström, showing the jultomten she popularized.

Snow on the roofs is gleaming.
All but the goblin are dreaming.

Gray he stands at the barnyard door,
Gray by the drifts of white there,
Looks, as oft he has looked before,
Up at the moon so bright there;
Looks at the woods, where the fir-trees tall
Shut the grange in with their dusky wall;
Ponders——some problem vexes,
Some strange riddle perplexes——

Passes his hand o'er beard and hair,
Shaking his head and cap then:
"Nay, that riddle's too hard, I swear,
I'll ne'er guess it mayhap then."
But, as his wont is, he soon drives out
All such thoughts of disturbing doubt,
Frees his old head of dizziness,
And turns him at once to business.

First he tries if the locks are tight,
Safe against every danger.
Each cow dreams in the pale moonlight
Summer dreams by her manger.
Dobbin, forgetful of bits that gall,
Dreams like the cows in his well-filled stall,

Leaning his neck far over
Armfuls of fragrant clover.

Then through the bars he sees the sheep,
Watches how well they slumber,
Eyes the cock on his perch asleep,
Round him hens without number.
Carlo wakes at the goblin's tread,
Wags then his tail and lifts his head;
Well acquainted the two are,
Friends that both tried and true are.

Last the goblin slips in to see
How all the folk are faring.
Long have they known how faithfully
He for their weal is caring.
Treading lightly on stealthy toes,
Into the children's room he goes,
Looks at each tiny treasure:
That is his greatest pleasure.

So has he seen them, sire and son,
Year by year in that room there
Sleep first as children every one.
Ah, but whence did they come there?
This generation to that was heir,
Blossomed, grew old, and was gone——but where?

That is the hopeless, burning
Riddle ever returning.

Back to the barn he goes to rest,
Where he has fixed his dwelling
Up in the loft near the swallow's nest,
Sweet there the hay is smelling.
Empty the swallow's nest is now,
Back though he'll come when the grass and bough
Bud in the warm spring weather,
He and his mate together.

Always they twitter away about
Places through which they've travelled,
Caring naught for the goblin's doubt,
Though it were ne'er unravelled.
Through a chink in one of the walls
Moonlight on the old goblin falls,
White o'er his beard it wanders;
Still he puzzles and ponders.

Forest and field are silent all,
Frost their whole life congealing,
Save that the roar of the waterfall
Faintly from far is stealing.
Then the goblin, half in a dream,
Thinks it is Time's unpausing stream,

Wonders whither 'tis going,
And from what spring 'tis flowing.

Cold is the night, and still, and strange,
Stars they glitter and shimmer.
All yet sleep in the lonely grange
Soundly till morn shall glimmer.
Now sinks the moon in night profound;
Snow on the firs and pines around,
Snow on the roofs is gleaming.
All but the goblin are dreaming.

Rydberg's poem was like Sweden's version of "'Twas the Night Before Christmas." It was an annual holiday story shared around the fire, while people enjoyed their bowls of risgrynsgröt—a sticky sweet rice pudding. The risgrynsgröt is critical to the Tomte. All he asks for a year of service is for you to leave out a bowl of risgrynsgröt on Christmas Eve. It's the Tomte's favorite treat. If you neglect to leave out the bowl of rice pudding, he may leave you, and then you'll have no help.

Don't despair if you've never made risgrynsgröt before. The recipe is straightforward.

Risgrynsgröt

3 cups water
1½ cups short-grained rice
1 teaspoon salt
3 cups whole milk
1 cinnamon stick
1 teaspoon butter

3 tablespoons sugar
additional butter, ground
cinnamon, and brown
sugar, for garnish
1 almond

The Tomten enjoying their bowls of risgrynsgröt. Illustration by Jenny Nyström, c. 1900.

Boil the water in a heavy-bottomed pot, then add the rice and salt. Stir once, then cover. Simmer twenty minutes. When the rice is done, pour in half of the milk and add the cinnamon stick. Simmer on low for fifteen more minutes and stir occasionally. Gradually add the rest of the milk while stirring to keep the rice from sticking.

Mix in the butter and sugar to taste. After about forty-five minutes the porridge should be creamy in consistency. Remove from heat, pour into bowls, add a pat of butter, and sprinkle with cinnamon and brown sugar. Leave out a bowl by your doorstep on Christmas Eve for the Tomten.

You may have noticed the recipe calls for one almond. The almond is supposed to be slipped into the porridge after it's done, but before it's served. As bowlfuls are scooped out for all in attendance, everyone keeps a lookout for the lucky almond. If it's in your bowl, you may receive an extra present or some kind of extra treat.

I know leaving out a food offering at night may feel a little too Pagan for some people, but how many years have you been setting out milk and cookies for Santa?

To my fellow Christmas-celebrating parents out there, the Tomten probably sound eerily familiar. Anyone who has ever been about to blissfully drift off to sleep one evening a week or two before Christmas, only to lurch up wide awake at the realization that they forgot about the Elf on the Shelf will see a connection to the Scandinavian Tomten.

15

Père Fouettard

I n northern France and Belgium, there's a story they tell of a butcher long ago who ran low on meat, so he abducted three lost children, slipped them into the back of his butcher shop, sliced them up, and placed their meat in a salting tub. I mentioned in the Saint Nicholas chapter that this story would come up again. The French postscript to this legendary tale indicates that once the fixed-up children left the butcher shop, Saint Nicholas turned to the butcher and told him that for his inhuman crime, the butcher would have to work for him.

"No more slicing up children!" Saint Nicholas told the butcher.

Nicholas tells the butcher: "No more slicing up children. From now on, you will be my servant. We will call you Père Fouettard."

Père Fouettard translates to "Father Whipper." Like Belsnickel, Père Fouettard beats naughty boys and girls into submission so that they can get back on the good moral path and still get presents for Christmas. No longer a butcher, Père Fouettard takes delight in doling out the beatings at the request of his boss, Saint Nicholas. In the most extreme cases of naughtiness, Père Fouettard might even abduct the bad child, who won't be seen again.

In the region of northern France and Belgium, Saint Nicholas arrives on December 6, and he's often accompanied by his servant, Père Fouettard.

For help with understanding Father Whipper, I had the chance to sit down with Pauline Giorgetti. Giorgetti is thirty years old and works as a preschool teacher in her hometown of Thionville, France. I asked her what Père Fouettard meant to her.

"He's very scary," she said. "As a preschool teacher, I have to say that kids are really scared of Père Fouettard."

Giorgetti grew up with the Father Whipper tradition. She explained how Saint Nicholas and Père Fouettard arrived at her school together each year. "It caused a lot of anxiety," she said. "Because you didn't know if you would receive a gift from Saint Nicholas, or if Père Fouettard would take you away." It's a tradition she continues in her own classroom today.

You can't overstate how powerful this story and imagery must be to young French kids. I recall when my daughter, Sophie, was young, we would visit the website *PortableNorthPole.com,* where you can order a person-alized message from Santa Claus. As parents, we would enter her name, age, select some of her interests, and tick some boxes as to why we're so proud of her. We would then receive an email from Santa Claus. We'd click on that email in front of young Sophie and the video would start. And there was Santa, saying, "Hello, Sophie! I can't believe you're six years old now!" Santa would continue with his message, mentioning the specifics, and all the while Sophie was lighting up but also clasping her hands in front of her face and fidgeting anxiously because she knew what was coming next . . . judgment!

When Santa finished his personalized message, he would then point to a fancy-looking North Pole machine with lights and a screen, and pull a lever to see if Sophie was on the Nice List or the Naughty List. The lights flashed, and then—for what seemed like hours to her, but was only a few seconds—the screen jumped between Naughty and Nice until it honed in on the final decision . . . and then . . . and then . . . and then . . . *Nice!*

Père Fouettard as Father Whipper in this 19th-century postcard.

Sophie exhaled a huge sigh of relief. (My kid is a damn angel. There was no chance of her landing on the Naughty List, but she didn't know that.) She ran off content that it looked like she'd get some loot on Christmas Day. My wife and I would look at each other after this annual email and ask the rhetorical question: Is this fun or cruel? Still, it became a tradition in our home, stressful as it was, and we continued the torture year after year.

I can only imagine what Sophie would have gone through had she seen Saint Nicholas and Père Fouettard walking toward her, wondering which person she would have to face.

As for when Father Whipper first showed up in stories, some point to the Siege of Metz in 1552. The troops of Holy Roman Emperor Charles V had encircled the French city of Metz. The people of Metz created an effigy of the emperor and burned him for all to see. They called this effigy Père Fouettard. His face was blackened from burning.

However, Père Fouettard could also be based on Hans Trapp, who hails from Alsace in northeastern France.

Hans Trapp is known as the Christmas Cannibal Scarecrow because of what he likes to eat and the way he looks—gaunt, with tattered clothes, long hair, and a beard. Locals will tell you that way back in the fifteenth century, Hans Trapp was a rich and powerful Scrooge-like man from Alsace, France, who showed no mercy or kindness to his debtors, nor to his neighbors. The people of Alsace feared him for good reason. They'd cross the street to avoid walking by the nasty man, who wouldn't hesitate to raise his hand against a wayward child or beggar.

Soon, rumors began to circulate that Trapp was so hungry for more power and wealth that he made a deal with the Devil. And maybe he did, because he only seemed to get richer and meaner. Eventually word reached

"Hans Trapp accompanies the Christmas Maiden." Hand-colored woodcut of a 19th-century illustration.

all the way up to the pope, who excommunicated Hans Trapp, which enabled Alsace to confiscate his money and land.

Dejected and furious, Trapp escaped eastward into the nearby mountains of Germany, where he stewed and seethed. He built a crude, makeshift home where his hunger turned taboo. He longed to taste human flesh, and by Christmastime, he was ready to give in to his unholy desire. So Trapp stuffed his clothes with straw to disguise himself and stood as still as a scarecrow at the edge of farm fields by empty, lonely roads, waiting for a victim.

Finally, a young boy walked by, leading his sheep. That's when Trapp sprang to life and stabbed the boy through the heart with a sharp stick. He dragged the boy's corpse back to his mountain shack, sliced him into little pieces, and roasted the meat. With his mouth watering, Trapp raised a forkful of cooked flesh to his mouth. Just then, a lightning bolt zapped down from the heavens and vaporized him.

You may think that's the end of it, but you could be wrong. There's a reason parents keep telling his tale around Christmas. The Christmas Cannibal Scarecrow Hans Trapp, covered in a robe that's leaking straw, might still be lurking and hunting for his next child victim.

The folkloric tale of Hans Trapp is loosely based on a real-life knight named Hans von Trotha, who lived in the Palatinate region of Germany near the French and German border. Von Trotha lived from roughly 1450 to 1503 and was in command of two castles. He got into a land dispute with the church that turned ugly (spoiler: *no one* wins a land dispute against the church—they're undefeated). The local abbot couldn't see things von Trotha's way regarding where land lines should be drawn, so the knight built a dam to stop the water supply to the nearby town. The abbot struck back and had the dam destroyed. But when the dam was destroyed, the water flooded the village, ruining homes and businesses. Eventually the pope stepped in and excommunicated Hans von Trotha.

So from Hans von Trotha to Hans Trapp to Père Fouettard, we get an amalgam of men-turned-monsters who show up around Christmas and have become servants of Saint Nicholas. No matter which version you choose, Hans Trapp or Père Fouettard, each has shown his fortitude in killing children if necessary.

As Pauline Giorgetti put it, "Kids are more interested in the Saint Nicholas and Père Fouettard tradition here than Santa Claus, because they're not afraid of Santa Claus. If they get less presents from Santa, it's okay. But Saint Nicholas is here to judge."

16

Zwarte Piet

n my quest to explore every Yuletide monster I could find, Zwarte Piet made my early radar. How could he not? Like Belsnickel and Père Fouettard, Zwarte Piet, or Black Peter, accompanies Saint Nicholas to deal with naughty children, with lethal corporal punishment if necessary.

I struggled with including him in this book. I have included him because Black Peter hasn't been able to keep himself out of the news for the past decade or so. At the annual Christmas festivals in his home country of the Netherlands, Black Peter is portrayed by a white-skinned person in blackface, which is racist by any measuring stick you care to use.

What changed my perspective was having drinks with a Dutch mother and daughter duo I've known for a few years now. We were in the United Kingdom for a conference when I brought up Black Peter. Suddenly a look of disgust came over mother Mary's face. Her daughter, Elizabeth, gave me a look like I had just hit a nerve I didn't know I'd hit.

I brought up the racism and blackface. Mary and Elizabeth were both quick to tell me there's another side to the story. We'll get back to Mary and Elizabeth. Either way, Black Peter is dividing a country during a time of year that's supposed to bring people together.

First, the backstory.

Black Peter was born in 1850 when Dutch author Jan Schenkman wrote a children's book called *Sint Nikolaas en Zijn Knecht* (*Saint Nicholas and His Servant*). The "servant" isn't specifically named in the book, but he looks like a caricature of a Moor child as they were depicted in seventeenth- and eighteenth-century paintings—with skin that's quite dark, wearing harem pants in the first edition, though in later printings he wears a colorful costume adorned with ruffles typical of sixteenth-century pages. Schenkman's book was popular when it first published because this story evolved the legend of Saint Nicholas into a saint more

The cover of Sint Nikolaas en Zijn Knecht (Saint Nicholas and His Servant), *by Jan Schenkman, 1850, Amsterdam.*

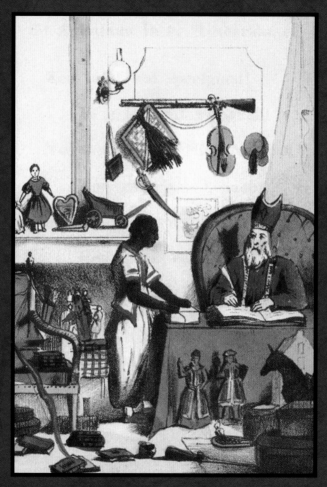

"Sinterclaus keeps a book," an illustration from Sint Nikolaas en Zijn Knecht *by* Jan Schenkman, 1850, *Amsterdam. In this depiction, the servant is not in blackface.*

focused on children and the poor, with Saint Nicholas using the latest technological innovations. This makes sense, considering the author was a schoolteacher from Amsterdam. Saint Nicholas was already the patron saint of the city, and Amsterdam was a hub of innovation. In Schenkman's book, he blends themes of old-time Saint Nicholas parties with new ones, like the saint arriving with his servant on a steamship from Spain, where he made the gifts. Then he departs on a hot-air balloon back to his native Turkey. Schenkman, like many who had come before him, wrote a new chapter into the story of Saint Nick.

To put Schenkman's book into the context of the day, in the nineteenth century, the Netherlands was still deeply involved in the slave trade. Some Dutch grew wealthy selling human beings to the United States or to Dutch colonies. Some Dutch nobles would "gift" a slave child to their other noble friends. Those children would become house servants and maybe treated as something like a pet and status symbol. The act is despicable by any modern standard, yet at the time, not everyone agreed on how human beings should be treated. Dark-skinned people from Africa, as well as indigenous people from other lands who lived in nature, were seen as "savages." They lacked culture, education, and religion, by European standards, so they must be less-than. As soon as you think of another group of people as something less than you, there's no limit to how poorly you can treat them. The moment you cross that line of thinking you're greater than, you become the monster. Slavery wasn't abolished in the Netherlands until 1863, but by that time, Schenkman's book had established itself in the popular culture.

Just because slavery was abolished in the Netherlands doesn't mean society changed its views overnight. The idea that Saint Nicholas had a helper to deal with the naughty children was already well established in

A 1901 postcard showing St. Nicholas with a black, Krampus-like servant.

Europe. The Netherlands now had their own version. Over time, folklore took over.

Sometimes it's the folklore that's the monster.

In the Netherlands, Saint Nicholas arrives on December 5—the eve of Saint Nicholas Feast Day. As early as 1800, the Dutch Saint Nicholas had a servant or page who accompanied him on his gift-giving rounds. But that servant was depicted as a white, dignified, and formal man wearing a wig, like a butler one might have on an estate.

Sometime on or just before December 5, Dutch children place their shoes in front of the fireplace. Saint Nicholas travels on his horse over the rooftops, delivering toys. Some kids will leave out straw, carrots, and water near their shoes for the horse. Black Peter then enters the house through the chimney to drop presents in the shoes.

To keep the tradition, but lose the racism, some Dutch have evolved Zwarte Piet into *Schoorsteen Piet*, or "Chimney Pete." This version of Pete has him in a different costume, with a face covered in soot, *not* blackface. Just a dirty man who spends a lot of time in chimneys. Schoorsteen Piet doesn't appease all of the anti–Zwarte Piet crowd, but dropping characters in blackface is a giant leap forward.

It's tragic when protestors find the need to attend holiday parades to call attention to something so overtly racist as Black Peter characters in blackface. What's worse is that there are those digging in on the issue. Some cry, "It's tradition and should carry on!" Likewise, the issue has drawn white supremacists to these same parades, carrying neo-Nazi flags and offering Nazi salutes to Zwarte Piet.

If irony had a patron saint, perhaps it would also be Saint Nicholas. Because the real Nicholas of Myra had dark, olive skin and brown eyes.

How do we know? In 2004, University of Manchester anthropologist Caroline Wilkinson took part in a BBC Two documentary called *The Real Face of Santa*. Using some of the remains taken from Nicholas's crypt in Myra, Wilkinson concluded Nicholas would have stood about five feet, six inches, had olive skin, dark brown eyes, and a wide chin and brow. They also found he had a broken nose and would have been built more like a bar bouncer. It's likely he would have worn a beard, considering that's what religious leaders of his time did.

Back to the Dutch duo of Elizabeth Koert, age forty-one, and her mother, Mary Vallo, who is seventy-three. Both white. As in other European countries, Saint Nicholas and Santa Claus are two different people who arrive on different days. Saint Nicholas arrives with Black Peter on December 5, the eve of Saint Nicholas Day, and Santa arrives on December 25. Elizabeth explains:

> When I was a kid, it was the eighties. Back then, it was full-on Black Pete with the ruffles and the hat and the feather, and big hooped earrings. There wasn't so much worry about whether or not it was culturally inappropriate, or if it was racist or anything like that. The whole discussion about blackface wasn't as alive in the eighties as it is today. I think there's a lot of misunderstanding about the reason behind Black Pete.

Koert told me about a school report she did back in middle school on Black Pete. (It helps that her uncle once published a book on Saint Nicholas and Black Peter.) She said the early helpers of Saint Nicholas weren't necessarily Moorish or even African. They were also South American, and many had white skin. They had dirty, sooty faces from traveling down

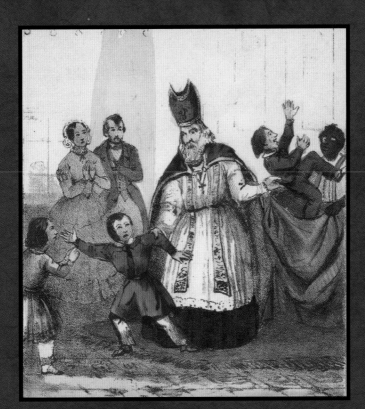

Zwarte Piet stuffing the bad children into a sack. An illustration from Sint Nikolaas en Zijn Knecht *by Jan Schenkman, 1850, Amsterdam.*

chimneys to deliver toys or to snatch up the naughty children. Black Peter offers presents but is also ready to dole out the punishment or even abduct naughty kids, if need be.

That's when Vallo jumped into the discussion. "The bad kids were supposed to be put in a bag, and they made a journey back to Spain, where Saint Nicholas is supposed to live," she said. "Nobody knows what happens to those kids. Were they made slaves? Were they reeducated? Nobody knows and nobody talks about it."

Not knowing somehow makes it worse, doesn't it? Sometimes death is better than the unknown.

Koert said the Saint Nicholas parades still happen in Amsterdam and in various communities around the Netherlands. And there are still Black Petes in blackface in some of those parades. There will be protestors on one side and supporters on the other. Sometimes it's up to the individual communities if they will allow Black Peter in blackface; sometimes it's left to parade organizers. Koert said:

There's still the traditional all blackface Petes, there's the Chimney Petes with dirty faces, there's Rainbow Petes with all colors of the rainbow: one with a blue face, one with a red face, one with an orange face; all the colors, just to make sure that it's diverse and not perceived as racist. But still wanting to try and hang on to the celebration itself. The celebration shouldn't be about racism, it should be about bringing children joy.

This gets to the heart of it. Elizabeth and Mary don't want to see the celebration go away because of Black Peter. They're fine with the Rainbow

Petes or Chimney Petes, but to stop the whole thing feels to them like cancel culture run amok. At the same time, it's tragic considering a strong police presence is needed at holiday parades in case there's a race riot.

If Black Peter was created as a new tradition in 1850, there's no rule to say that he can't change again—that Zwarte Piet can't be replaced by Schoorsteen Piet, or even Zwarte Krampus, as the servant of Saint Nicholas. As for what happens to the naughty children dragged off in bags to Spain . . . I prefer to leave that a horrible mystery.

17

La Befana

hat's a scary holiday without its witches? Though my family heritage is not Italian, there's a Yuletide witch who hails from Italy that I would love to adopt. Her name is La Befana.

Today, La Befana is an old, ugly hag of a woman, but inside lies a heart of gold. However, there was a time when her exterior was just as beautiful as her interior. Befana arrives on January 5, the Eve of Epiphany, and fills the socks or shoes of good children with candy and toys. The naughty kids receive lumps of coal, onions, or garlic. But we've heard that candy-and-toys-in-stockings part before, from other Christmas-bringers. What sets Befana apart is that after delivering her goodies to the children, she's been known to clean your house before she departs. Sign. Me. Up.

The Christian version of Befana's origin dates back to the three magi following a star toward the birthplace of Jesus. En route, the magi get lost and find themselves at the doorstep of La Befana. They ask the old woman if she knows the way to find the Son of God, but she does not. However, La Befana offers the three wise men lodging for the night. Her home is the cleanest and most comfortable in the village, after all. The magi marvel at what an immaculate housekeeper the Befana is, and what a kind host.

Come morning, the magi invite Befana to join them in their quest to find the baby Jesus, but the old woman declines, saying she has too much housework. The magi shrug and are soon on their way to Bethlehem. Later that evening, the Befana has an epiphany that she should have gone with the three wise men, but it's too late. She searches, but she can't find the magi, or the baby Jesus. So to this day the Befana continues her search, bearing gifts for all of the good children.

Like many traditions and customs associated with this holiday, this backstory lays a Christian veneer over a Pagan custom. In his 1823 book, *Vestiges of Ancient Manners and Customs, Discoveries in Modern Italy and Sicily*, the

Befana's been known to use the broom she rode in on to clean your house before she departs.
German Christmas card, 1920.

Reverend John Blunt describes Befana celebrations he witnessed in Florence. First, Blunt describes how the children hung their stockings on the Eve of Epiphany, and how those stockings were filled with "cakes, comfits, and other dolci" that the children delighted in discovering come the morning. Blunt continues:

> I should add, that the orgies of this supernatural personage [Befana] are celebrated as soon as it grows dark, by parties dressed in burlesque costumes running about the town . . . with torches in their hands, singing, shouting, and blowing glass-horns. Sometimes again they mount carts adorned with boughs, and glaring with flambeaux; and, without sparing either the horse in the shafts, or the crowd in the streets, they drive furiously over the pavement the greater part of the night.

The drunken revelry also sounds familiar, no? Blunt continues:

The Beffana [*sic*] appears to be heir at law of a certain heathen goddess called Strenia, who presided over the new-year's gifts, Strenæ, from which, indeed, she derived her name . . . Her presents were of the same description as those of the Beffana [*sic*]—figs, dates, and honey . . . Moreover, her solemnities were vigorously opposed by the early Christians on account of their noisy, riotous, and licentious character.

Christians didn't like the Befana with her Pagan roots, and they tried to stop her, but they couldn't. So they did the only thing left that they could do. They revised her backstory to give it a Christian spin related to wise men and the birth of Jesus. But like a bad hair bleaching, Befana's roots shine through.

In ancient Rome, Strenia was the goddess of the new year. Romans would exchange *strenæ*, or gifts of good omens—gifts like coins, sweet breads, and figs—for the coming year. The New Year was a time of purification, protection, pleasure, rebirth, and cleaning out.

Strenia, or Strenua, *goddess of the new year.*

La Befana, *by Bartolomeo Pinelli, 1821.*

The goddess Strenia was depicted as a beautiful and youthful, even alluring, woman. She had her own grove of trees near the top of Via Sacra, the main thoroughfare of ancient Rome. On the New Year, twigs from her grove were carried through the streets in a parade to the citadel. Recall how Reverend Blunt observed carts covered in boughs—or tree branches—racing through the streets of 1820s' Florence. The connection to the old ways wasn't quite severed yet.

I spoke to Frederic Berruti about La Befana. He's fifty-four years old and currently lives in Michigan, but was born in Genoa in northern Italy. He moved north to Turino, Italy, when he was five. He grew up with the Befana tradition. He said La Befana was not nearly as big a deal as Christmas Day when he was a kid. But he recalls placing his shoes under the Christmas tree on the Eve of Epiphany. He would also leave out either a cookie and some milk, or an orange or mandarin and some wine as an offering to La Befana. "In the morning we'd look under the tree where I put my shoe, and La Befana would always put a little extra gift in there," Berruti said. Gifts like a book, some kind of trinket. "It's like Santa, but a Santa redux," he said. A second chance for kids who didn't get everything on their wish list.

He said after Epiphany, the Christmas tree came down, the holidays were over, and it was time to clean up. For some parents, La Befana presented one more holiday task to finish before starting the new year.

These old gods and goddesses have no place in the brave, new monotheistic world of the Common Era. While we've almost lost the names of the old gods, their traditions and ways survive. What's a tradition anyway, other than a recurring habit? Still, it's this habit that connects us to our parents, our parents' parents, and so on down the line. Over centuries, Strenia was made ugly and hag-like, they called her Befana, and then they gave her a Christian backstory. However, her spirit survives, and I'm sure she's grateful for the wine left by the shoes under the tree.

18

The Karakoncolos

he same region that gave us Saint Nicholas also gave us a shape-shifting, subterranean, nocturnal, riddle-asking, Yuletide beast of a creature called Karakoncolos. He's the Christmas Bigfoot—if Bigfoot lurked in towns and villages around the holidays trying to trick his way into your home, or ride on your back until dawn.

Karakoncolos tunnels in the underground and slinks through the shadows of Serbia, Greece, Albania, Bosnia, Cyprus, Turkey, Bulgaria, and Macedonia, but makes his way into town come Christmas. During daylight hours, you're safe, but once the sun sets, this tricky beast rises aboveground and could be anywhere or look like anyone.

His name is spelled various ways depending on the country, but for the sake of ease, I'm going to stick with the Turkish spelling, in honor of Saint Nicholas's home country. I beg the forgiveness of other regions where he hunts under a slightly different moniker.

Look out. He's a shape-shifter.

In his natural state, Karakoncolos is a dark, hairy monster with goat-like legs. Sometimes he's depicted with horns, other times with tusks like a boar. He may have ears like a donkey and sport glowing red eyes. He's a monster. By his description, you'd think he'd be easy enough to avoid. If you walked down a street one evening and saw some beast looking like Karakoncolos, you'd need no prodding to run for your life. But few people see this monster in his natural state and live to tell about it, because he's a shape-shifter. He can look and sound like anyone, so don't trust your eyes or ears.

Why Christmas? Though we can't know the mind of a monster, we can speculate. In Serbia, the Twelve Days of Christmas were once referred to as "unbaptized days," an unholy time when demonic forces were most active. People avoid going out late at night for fear of drawing the attention of evil.

January 1 on the Julian calendar is January 14 on the Gregorian calendar, a day called "Little Christmas" in this region, when the danger is most high. So on Little Christmas Eve, a group of seven, nine, or eleven unmarried men called *Sirovari* chase away demons for the safety of others. The reason for the specific number is that it's believed if the number of *Sirovari* is even, then one of them will die within the year. So, odd it is. The *Sirovari* run through the streets ringing loud bells, rattles, party ratchets (those annoying cog rattle instruments we often see—or, rather, *hear*—at New Year's Eve celebrations), and dragging horseshoes tied to a rope. As loud as they can, they yell out, "*Sirovo burovo!*"

The *Sirovari* always shift position. They hide, then reappear, so no one can count them. Though they're loud and noisy, people in the village are happy to hear and greet them because of their valuable service of chasing away the demons. The *Sirovari* are welcomed into homes, where they're given food and drink before being sent on their way.

With demons around, so is the Karakoncolos. This devilish creature lurks during the Twelve Days of Christmas. In Turkey, the creature hunts during the ten days of *Zemheri*, which roughly translates to the "dreadful cold." On the coldest days of winter the Karakoncolos stands in shadowy street corners asking passersby questions so as not to draw attention to himself. As a shape-shifter, the monster can look like an ordinary person, or even one of your relatives. If you suspect the stranger in the shadow who just asked you some innocuous question may be a Karakoncolos, you must be sure that the word "black" is in your reply. ("Kara" means black in

Turkish.) If you don't use the word "black" in your answer, the Karakoncolos will strike you down with a mighty blow.

Other Karakoncolos attacks start off eerily familiar . . . you may hear a relative calling out to you. You're *certain* it's their voice, so you reply. But then you fall into a trance. That's when the Karakoncolos leaps onto your back and rides you like a horse wherever he chooses to go until morning. When the sun rises, the beast must get back belowground until the sun sets again, and you're left exhausted, but thankfully still alive.

In some parts of Serbia, the Karakoncolos perches himself above your home's door, waiting for someone to sneak out at night. Usually those sneaking out are adulterers heading for a rendezvous with their paramours, or heading to the local brothel. As soon as the person sneaks outside, the Karakoncolos leaps onto their back and lashes them with a stick, or digs his claws into their back and rides them through the forest until dawn, when he must go down below again.

All monsters serve the needs of the time and community where they lurk, whether to keep people safe inside their homes during the coldest and darkest parts of winter, or to remind us not to trust a stranger, or to stay loyal to our spouses.

Still, some risks aren't worth taking. This Christmas, when annoying Aunt Ethel knocks at your front door holding that awful casserole, it could be her . . . or it could be the shape-shifting Karakoncolos trying to lure you to open your door. I say don't risk it. Leave Ethel outside just in case.

19

Santa Claus

ur modern concept of Santa Claus may have gotten its start with Nicholas of Myra, but the tree that sprouted from that early seed doesn't look much like the original anymore. Santa Claus is a mix of many influences. Like the monsters of this holiday, he takes the form and shape of what's needed at the time.

Saint Nicholas's evolution into our modern Santa Claus occurred during the Industrial Revolution. Which is *not* a coincidence. Many of the ghouls and monsters we've explored so far rose to prominence during this same period. Also *not* a coincidence.

In the bleakest days of Midwinter, people need a good guy.

The Industrial Revolution began in 1760. But, before we go there, draw your mind back to a place a century or two before 1760, when most people lived in small towns. Regular folks would have a few animals to provide food, and they would grow some crops. In towns, everyone's job would be organized by guilds or town rules that governed who could trade what with whom. Prices for goods and services were fixed.

Some people had specialized jobs, such as smiths, or barrel makers, or cobblers, or any other occupations that required a skilled hand. But the cobbler could only make a pair of shoes so quickly.

There were some machines in this era. There were stone mills powered by wind, mules, or waterwheels placed on a stream, river, or lake runoff. So the idea that a wheel could drive a machine already existed, but the machines were crude. By the second half of the eighteenth century, however, the world was about to change in ways and speeds it had never seen before. In 1764, James Hargreaves of Stanhill, England, invented the spinning jenny for turning cotton into cloth. A single worker could manage eight or nine spools at once, whereas before he could only manage one. An eightfold increase in productivity is staggering. Of course, these were just the early days. Soon, other automations would provide a hundredfold increase in productivity. Factories emerged in and around cities, because that's where the labor force lived. And in a very short period of time, the world had changed forever.

People living in rural farming villages sent their children off to the cities for factory work. Though the conditions were often abysmal in some of these factories, where owners cared more about their profits and productivity than they did about people's fingers, arms, limbs, or lives, it was still a chance to make something new of oneself.

It was a confusing and frightening time. There were so many new sights and sounds. So much was changing so fast. If you were going to get ahead, you needed to be educated, which meant more information coming at you at every turn. Higher literacy rates meant more newspapers, books, and periodicals. Information sharing meant more innovation. But also information overload! Humans had never before been subjected to so much information so fast. People were confused, scared, and excited living in this brave new world. But that fear made people want to latch on to something old, something primal that spoke to the simpler times. From there, the monsters emerged from the shadows of legend and lore, but so too did the angels and good guys. In the bleakest days of Midwinter, people found that they needed a good guy. They needed Santa Claus.

The Dutch brought *Sinterklaas* with them to New Amsterdam in the 1600s, but those early settlers aligned with the Dutch Reformed Church, which very much shared the Puritans' thoughts on Christmas—that it's *not* a thing. When the British occupied New Amsterdam in 1660, they promptly renamed the town New York, and the Dutch became a minority influence. Santa Claus, and the notion of Christmas, would lie dormant for more than a century and a half.

When the Industrial Revolution began to transform the world starting in 1760, society changed at a pace never before seen in all of human history. As with any new revolution, this one took a few decades to ramp up around the world. One innovator built upon another innovator until it seemed like anything was possible, from powered ships to flying balloon ships, to sending telegraphed messages almost instantly across entire nations.

Author and Christmas-collector Jock Elliot called the time period from 1823 to 1848 the "Big Bang of Christmas." Amid the socioeconomic gap and dizzying new innovations, Santa Claus emerged from the maelstrom. There's a strong case that he was born in New York long before he moved to the North Pole.

In 1809, New Yorker Washington Irving penned *Knickerbocker's History of New York*. A work of satire, the book looked at contemporary New York life. Irving's fiction claimed that Saint Nicholas inspired early prominent Dutch settler Oloffe Van Kortlandt to build a city. Irving offers:

> And the sage Oloffe dreamed a dream—and, lo! the good St. Nicholas came riding over the tops of the trees, in that self-same wagon wherein he brings his yearly presents to children . . . And he lit his pipe by the fire, and sat himself down and smoked; and as he smoked the smoke from his pipe ascended into the air, and spread like a cloud overhead. And Oloffe bethought him, and he hastened and climbed

up to the top of one of the tallest trees, and saw that the smoke spread over a great extent of country—and as he considered it more attentively he fancied that the great volume of smoke assumed a variety of marvelous forms, where in dim obscurity he saw shadowed out palaces and domes and lofty spires, all of which lasted but a moment, and then faded away, until the whole rolled off, and nothing but the green woods were left. And when St. Nicholas had smoked his pipe he twisted it in his hatband, and laying his finger beside his nose, gave the astonished Van Kortlandt a very significant look, then mounting his wagon, he returned over the treetops and disappeared.

And Van Kortlandt awoke from his sleep greatly instructed, and he aroused his companions, and related to them his dream, and interpreted it that it was the will of St. Nicholas that they should settle down and build the city here.

Flying through the air in his wagon . . . laying a finger beside his nose . . . all familiar Santa Claus traits. Evolutions are often slow, but on occasion, they make leaps. Like Santa's did on December 6, 1810, when wealthy New York merchant, prominent citizen, and philanthropist John Pintard held a banquet in honor of Saint Nicholas on Saint Nicholas Day. He even commissioned a poster depicting Saint Nicholas—because every holiday needs a face. Below the image of bald and pious-looking Saint Nicholas is a poem. On the left side it's written in Dutch. On the right is its English translation.

Saint Nicholas, good holy man!
Put on the Tabard, best you can,
Go, clad therewith, to Amsterdam,
From Amsterdam to Hispanje,
Where apples bright of Oranje,
And likewise those granate surnam'd,

St. NICHOLAS.
Dec. 6th. A.D.343.

SANCTE CLAUS, goed heylig Man!
Trek uwe beste Tabaert aen,
Reis daer me'e na Amsterdam,
Van Amsterdam na 'Spanje,
Daer Appelen van Oranje,
Daer Appelen van granaten,
Die rollen door de Straaten.
SANCTE CLAUS, myn goede Vriend!
Ik heb U allen tyd gedient,
Wille U my nu wat geven,
Ik zal U dienen alle myn Leven.

SAINT NICHOLAS, good holy man!
Put on the Tabard,* best you can,
Go, clad therewith, to Amsterdam,
From Amsterdam to Hispanje,
Where apples *bright* † of Oranje,
And likewise those *granate* ‡ surnam'd,
Roll through the streets, all free unclaim'd.
SAINT NICHOLAS, my dear good friend!
To serve you ever was my end,
If you will, now, me something give,
I'll serve you ever while I live.

    * Kind of Jacket.   † Oranges.   ‡ Pomegranates.

St. Nicholas. *by John Pintard, 1810.*

Roll through the streets, all free unclaim'd.
Saint Nicholas, my dear good friend!
To serve you ever was my end,
If you will, now, me something give,
I'll serve you ever while I live.

There it is. Saint Nicholas arriving in Amsterdam from Spain with treats like apples, oranges, and pomegranates. However, the more curious piece of this poster is the Dutch translation on the left. "Saint Nicholas" should read *Sinterklaas*. But it doesn't. Pintard wrote "SANTTE CLAUS."

Pintard was growing concerned with the plight of the poor. Consider this: In 1760, the population of New York City was about eighteen thousand people. In 1810 the population swelled to seventy-two thousand. That's a fourfold increase in fifty years. New York was getting crowded, with more people vying for jobs that paid very little. The masses were getting unruly, but Pintard thought of a solution: bring back the old ways of Christmas when the rich and the poor would feast together. However, the old ways of Saturnalia and Yule were unheard of in the United States, so he tried his best to invent new traditions. Which may sound preposterous until you consider all traditions were invented at some point. Pintard was trying to build off something ancient that he hoped still resided in our DNA.

The Santa Claus winds were swirling during the first half of the nineteenth century. The idea was already there, the holiday was there, but who would be the face of it?

On Christmas Eve 1822, Dr. Clement Moore, a teacher, scholar, and poet, was struck with the answer. Dr. Moore lived on a ninety-four-acre farm called Chelsea in New York (today, this section of New York City is still called Chelsea). On Christmas Eve, he was driven in a sleigh into the city to buy a Christmas turkey when he began composing some lines to a whimsical little poem. When he returned to his farm with the turkey, he wrote it all down and read it Christmas Day. A family member liked the poem so much, she wrote down a copy and mailed it to the *Troy Sentinel* newspaper in upstate New York. With no name to go with the poem, the *Troy Sentinel* published it under "Anonymous" on December 23, 1823.

The poem would go on to be published in two almanacs and countless other newspapers each Christmas. Today the lines are so familiar, I only have to give you the first two and you can likely continue them in your head:

> *'Twas the night before Christmas, when all thro' the house,*
> *Not a creature was stirring, not even a mouse;*

Moore considered himself a scholar and serious poet. He was embarrassed by the popularity of "A Visit from St. Nicholas." It took twenty years for him to put his name back on the piece in a collection of his poems that published in 1844.

Though this poem only refers to the main character as St. Nicholas and never uses "Santa" once, it defined this Yuletide figure who had previously lacked definition. Building off Washington Irving (even borrowing the line about laying his finger beside his nose), Moore told us that St. Nicholas is a right jolly old elf, with a big belly, who comes down the chimney with toys, then flies off in a sled pulled by flying reindeer named Dasher, Dancer, Prancer, Vixen, Comet, Cupid, Dunder, and Blixem. (Those last two are spelled as they were in the *Troy Sentinel* back in 1823—some have argued they were typos in the newspaper.)

Santa, *by Thomas Nast, 1863, for* Harper's Weekly.

He's a right jolly old elf.

Throughout the coming decades, the legend of Santa Claus grew through poems, stories, songs, and practices. The jolly old elf was catching on. But his look began to take form on January 3, 1863, when Bavaria-born cartoonist Thomas Nast drew a cartoon for *Harper's Weekly* depicting Santa Claus sitting on a sleigh pulled by reindeer, distributing gifts to soldiers in the Union Army. In the picture, Santa has a big, white beard, and his round physique is clad in a furry suit depicting stars and stripes, so there's no confusion as to which army he favors during these times of Civil War in the United States.

Over the next twenty-three years, Nast would go on to illustrate Santa Claus thirty-two more times for *Harper's Weekly*. Each time, Santa's look evolved slightly. His 1881 image titled *Merry Old Santa Claus* is perhaps his most famous and looks most familiar to us in modern times.

From here, we leap fifty years into the future. Go ahead and crack open a Coca-Cola, because in 1931, America is still stuck in Prohibition. There's no rum to add to that fizzy soda pop—you'll have to drink it straight to drown your sorrows that we're also in the teeth of the Great Depression.

The stock market crashed in October of 1929, and Americans were struggling big time. I'm old enough to have lived through multiple recessions, even the Great Recession of 2007 to 2009. I know the general fear that can loom over us working folk like the Grim Reaper's scythe ready to sever us from our financial foundation during tough times. Economists tell us the only way out of a financial recession is to spend money. Crazy,

Merry Old Santa Claus, *by Thomas Nast, 1881.*

right?! If you lack money, how do you spend what you don't have? And if you have money, and you see the world crumbling around you, every instinct tells you to hoard it. Because I've lived through a few recessions so far, it's clear the economists are correct. We just need a little prodding to part with our cash.

Enter Santa Claus. In 1931, Coca-Cola commissioned illustrator Haddon Sundblom to paint Santa Claus holding a Coke. Sundblom took his inspiration from Moore's poem "A Visit from St. Nicholas" and from Thomas Nast's illustrations. But the execs at Coca-Cola felt Nast's depiction of Santa showed him as too strict. Maybe even a little stiff. They wanted the jolliest of jolly elves. By this time, it was generally understood that Santa Claus was an older man with white hair and a big beard. But sometimes he'd wear a green coat (like the Ghost of Christmas Present in Charles Dickens's *A Christmas Carol*); other times he'd be depicted as looking kind of mean and judgmental, or tall and gaunt. Before Sundblom, Santa had yet to be codified.

Sundblom drew a rotund mountain of a man with rosy cheeks, a fur-trimmed red suit, and a red hat. Coca-Cola placed these Santa ads in *The Saturday Evening Post, Ladies' Home Journal, National Geographic, The New Yorker*, and a few other periodicals. And you know what? It worked. Coca-Cola sales boomed around the holidays in 1931. Depression be damned.

In following years, Coke's Santa would sometimes be shown wearing his red hat. At first, it may have looked like some sort of nightcap, but as it laid over on its side, it formed a kind of triangle, like a bishop's mitre (something Saint Nicholas would have worn in his day).

In the years that followed, Coca-Cola continued to use Santa to sell Coke during the holidays. People looked forward to each year's ads—bright spots in otherwise bleak years. But soon, other companies and retailers took note. And that's when something profound occurred to everyone who sold something in the United States: *Coca-Cola didn't own Santa Claus!* They too could use this jolly old elf to sell their products and services. Imagine if you could get the world's biggest celebrity to endorse your product, whether you were a local donut shop or a national car manufacturer . . . for free?! Sign us up, right?

The day after Thanksgiving in the United States has become known as Black Friday, because it's the day that retailers hope to go into the black on their accounting spreadsheets. The day they hope to turn profitable for the year, making December all profit. If people spend their money to get the latest and greatest toys, clothes, jewelry, perfume, or whatever else their heart desires, retailers make money, everyone in the supply chain hires more people to keep up, and the economy keeps truckin' down the highway, led by a jolly old man in a red suit driving a sleigh pulled by reindeer.

By 1939, America was out of the Great Depression. And Santa had become a permanent fixture in our culture. On December 26, 1941, President Franklin Roosevelt signed a bill into law that Thanksgiving would henceforth be held on the fourth Thursday of November. Before 1941, Thanksgiving was held on the last Thursday of November, per President Abraham Lincoln. Why the change? Because retailers noted that it didn't always leave enough shopping time before Christmas. What's good for the economy is good for America, so FDR made the change, and we've been camping out at retailers the day after Thanksgiving for doorbuster sales ever since.

By the 1930s, Santa had become so prominent and important that all of his cohorts, helpers, and henchmen had to be pushed far back into the shadows.

The Yuletide monsters wait in the shadows . . .

Christmas became a time to spend money and help the economy, and there was simply no room for anything dark or consequential. Those monsters who accompanied Saint Nicholas didn't die, though . . . they waited patiently in the shadows until they were needed again. Until they were summoned.

20

Marley's Ghost

arley was dead: to begin with. There's no doubt whatever about that." So Charles Dickens begins his masterpiece *A Christmas Carol.* "This must be distinctly understood, or nothing wonderful can come of the story I am going to relate."

A Christmas Carol is a story I consume every holiday season. Either by rereading my well-worn copy of the book, watching some of the many movie versions of the story (my favorite being the 1951 black-and-white version starring Alastair Sim), or watching it performed live on stage. Whether Muppets or animated characters are rendering this tale, I'm in, because the power of this story shines through, no matter the medium.

So much of our modern understanding of what this holiday is supposed to mean is derived from this powerful ghost story. Before Charles Dickens published this book in 1843, Christmas in England was not a big holiday. In the United States, even less so. Kids had to attend school, and most working-class people still had to toil.

Dickens could see the gap widening between the rich and the poor during his lifetime. After traveling extensively in the United States, he returned home to England and vowed not to return to the United States so long as slavery was still legal. His travelogue and critique on slavery, *American Notes,* did *not* win Dickens many fans in the United States when it was published in October of 1842. So when *A Christmas Carol* came out a year later in December 1843, it wasn't a hit in the United States like it was in England, where the story began to haunt London in the best possible way.

Back in the United States, a storm was brewing. A mighty storm that would build into the Civil War between 1861 and 1865. With slavery being the heart of the cause, America was reckoning with its original sin. In the end, 620,000 people lost their lives in the line of duty. As America was trying to put its broken self back together again, Charles

Dickens knew what we needed. With slavery abolished, Charles Dickens once again boarded a ship bound for Boston, where he checked in to the Parker House Hotel on November 19, 1867. Christmas in New England was hardly celebrated when Dickens arrived. But Dickens knew the power of his "ghostly little book," as he refers to it in his preface. He'd seen it transform audiences in England, and he was ready to do the same for America.

Bah! Humbug!

After rehearsing the reading of his book over and over in front of a mirror that still hangs in the Omni Parker House Hotel today—a mirror where they say you can occasionally still catch a glimpse of the famous author's ghost—Dickens took *A Christmas Carol* to the Tremont Temple stage in Boston on December 3. Dickens read. The audience sat rapt until the very end.

Dickens's manager at the time, George Dolby, observed in his 1885 book, *Charles Dickens as I Knew Him*:

When at last the Reading of The Carol was finished, and the final words had been delivered, and "so, as Tiny Tim observed, God bless us every one," a dead silence seemed to prevail—a sort of public sigh as it were—only to be broken by cheers and calls, the most enthusiastic and uproarious, causing Mr. Dickens to break through his rule, and again presenting himself before his audience, to bow his acknowledgments.

A Boston factory owner named Mr. Fairbanks attended one of these early readings by Dickens and was so moved he decided to close down his factory on Christmas Day, and he sent a turkey to each of his employees.

Dickens left his mark on the dining-table landscape of Christmas dinner too. Before his story, the goose was the go-to bird of choice. As one writer in the December 21, 1867, *Wilke's Spirit of the Times* newspaper wrote, "Dickens' *Christmas Carol* helps the poultry business amazingly. Everybody who read it and who has money immediately rushes off and buys a turkey for the poor."

A Christmas Carol unfolds the tale of Ebenezer Scrooge,

> a squeezing, wrenching, grasping, scraping, clutching, covetous, old sinner! Hard and sharp as flint, from which no steel had ever struck out generous fire; secret, and self-contained, and solitary as an oyster . . . He carried his own low temperature always about with him; he iced his office in the dog-days; and didn't thaw it one degree at Christmas.

You know the type.

Scrooge's business partner Jacob Marley had died seven Christmases ago on that very night. While others intend to make merry and spread good cheer and charity, Scrooge will have none of it. Because, for most of his adult life, he never has had any patience for that which doesn't financially profit him in some way. Christmas is indeed a humbug to Scrooge.

Scrooge doesn't even have time for what little family he has left. When his nephew, Fred, barges in to Scrooge's countinghouse to extend an invitation to Christmas dinner, Scrooge dismisses him with a declaration of "Humbug." But Dickens, through Fred, delivers his message of what the holiday is supposed to mean. Fred tells his Uncle Scrooge:

I have always thought of Christmas time, when it has come round . . . as a good time; a kind, forgiving, charitable, pleasant time; the only time I know of, in the long calendar of the year, when men and women seem by one consent to open their shut-up hearts freely, and to think of people below them as if they really were fellow-passengers to the grave, and not another race of creatures bound on other journeys. And therefore, uncle, though it has never put a scrap of gold or silver in my pocket, I believe that it *has* done me good, and *will* do me good; and I say, God bless it!

That Christmas Eve, back at home—the very home once occupied by Scrooge's dead business partner before it was bequeathed—Scrooge catches a vision in his door knocker. Was that glowing face Jacob Marley? No. It couldn't be. Scrooge shakes off the spooky vision, hurries himself upstairs, and sets himself by a meager fire to eat a bowl of gruel. Mid-slurp, the chamber bell mounted by the door catches Scrooge's attention. It swings slowly at first, then begins to peal out mighty rings, as does every bell in the house. The bells stop as quickly as they began. Silence is followed by a dreadful thump from somewhere deep within the house. *Thump. Thump.* The sound of chains dragging on the floor follows until the chamber door flies open, and Scrooge stares wide-eyed at the ghost of his seven-years-dead business partner, Jacob Marley.

At first, Scrooge refuses to believe his senses. Yet, there before him stands the ghost of Marley. "The chain he drew was clasped about his middle," Dickens wrote. "It was long, and wound about him like a tail; and it was made (for Scrooge observed it closely) of cash-boxes, keys, padlocks, ledgers, deeds, and heavy purses wrought in steel."

The two sit together—man and ghost—for the most important conversation of Scrooge's life. Marley laments that he wasted his existence

Marley's Ghost, by J. Leech. 1843.

pursuing only financial profit, that he wears the chain he forged in life: "I made it link by link, and yard by yard; I girded it on of my own free will, and of my own free will I wore it." Marley says that Scrooge's own chain was just as long seven years ago, but Scrooge has toiled on it ever since. It's a ponderous chain.

Marley offers Scrooge but one chance of escaping this dreadful fate—a chance of Marley's procuring. He explains that Scrooge must be visited by three spirits. And somehow, after this most profound of ghostly encounters, Scrooge is able to get himself to sleep in his dark, cold bedchamber.

As the clock bell tolls one, a light illuminates his darkened room. There before Scrooge stands a spirit—a strange figure like a child, but also like an old man. Dressed in pure white, it holds a branch of fresh holly. The Ghost of Christmas Past takes Scrooge on a trip through his own childhood, back to his school days. Scrooge lights up with a smile, seeing children he used to know and recalling good times from his youth. Yet, there's sadness. A solitary schoolboy sits inside. A boy neglected by his family and friends at Christmas. The boy is young, lonely Ebenezer Scrooge.

The Ghost of Christmas Past takes Scrooge through his teen years, through falling in love with Belle and his apprenticeship at ole Fezziwig's—a time when Scrooge was happy and the world was full of possibilities. Yet Scrooge soon fell in love with something else: money. Knowing his heart was lost to her, Scrooge's fiancée, Belle, released him from his commitment. Scrooge met Marley, and two wolves found their purpose: making money at all costs. When Scrooge can take no more of watching his youthful self turn into a hardened man, he extinguishes the gentle spirit.

Next up, the jovial Ghost of Christmas Present. A giant of a man, bearded and clothed in a green robe bordered with fur. Beneath the garment, his bare feet. A holly wreath adorns his head, and an antique scabbard hangs from his waist, but it holds no sword. He invites Scrooge to know him better.

The Ghost of Christmas Present explains how he has many brothers. Over 1,800 of them! (More than 2,000 of them, if you update for today.) This spirit takes Scrooge on a tour through the present day. He shows Scrooge how others are celebrating the holiday, how a wave of his torch spreads good cheer to anyone it touches. Scrooge observes his nephew and his nephew's friends, his clerk, Bob Cratchit, and his family, especially poor Tiny Tim, with his crutch and illness, who won't survive if the future isn't altered with better care and food. Knowing that Scrooge himself has the means to help the Cratchits financially, so they can afford doctors and a better lifestyle—though he hasn't—gives Scrooge a moment of pause. And seeing poor miners celebrating the joy of the holidays despite having next to nothing makes Scrooge understand there's something he's missed about this Christmas holiday.

Before taking his leave, the Ghost of Christmas Present reveals beneath his robe two ragged children. When Scrooge asks who these children belong to, the spirit answers:

They are Man's. And they cling to me, appealing from their fathers.
This boy is Ignorance. This girl is Want. Beware them both . . . but
most of all beware this boy, for on his brow I see that written which
is Doom, unless the writing be erased.

With that, the church bell tolls midnight, the Ghost of Christmas Present disintegrates into ashes. However, lurking in the shadows is the very figure of Death itself, shrouded in deep black to hide all of the spirit's features. This spirit holds an outstretched hand, pointing the way for Scrooge to follow. The Ghost of Christmas Yet to Come reveals a cold and lonely future for Scrooge.

The Ghost of Christmas Present, by J. Leech. 1843.

The Ghost of Christmas Yet to Come, by J. Leech. 1843.

Scrooge witnesses flashes of scenes from his life. He sees important men of business vaguely referring to someone who has died, and how one says with a laugh that he doesn't care to attend the funeral service unless lunch is provided. He sees his laundress, his maid, and an undertaker at the pawnbroker selling simple items that seem vaguely familiar to Scrooge. But most disconcerting is the way the group laughs with the pawnbroker over the death of this man. It seems their attitude is that the world should be glad to be rid of him. Scrooge is appalled that no one grieves the loss of this man. The scene changes, and Scrooge sees the Cratchits' humble home, where Tiny Tim is gone and the family sits brokenhearted.

Then comes the frightful climax for Ebenezer Scrooge. The spirit whisks him to a frigid and dark boneyard and points ominously toward a headstone. Scrooge is shaking with fear, as if he already knows what's waiting for him. Still, he has his moment of reckoning. He asks the spirit, "Men's courses will foreshadow certain ends, to which, if persevered in, they must lead . . . But if the courses be departed from, the ends will change. Say it is thus with what you show me!"

The spirit doesn't speak. He simply points toward the stone in the ground, revealing the name: Ebenezer Scrooge.

Scrooge weeps, clawing at the dark robes of the frightening phantom, and suddenly wakes up in his bedchamber. It's Christmas morning. And everything has changed inside of Scrooge. He faced his demons and the ghosts and events from his own past that shaped him into a cold and bitter miser of a man. He's come through the other side redeemed. He sends a turkey feast to Bob Cratchit, he attends Christmas dinner with his nephew, and he delights in this happy new world he finds himself seeing for the first time with awakened eyes. He gives to charity, he raises his clerk's wages to help him with his family. "He became as good a friend, as good a master, and as good a man, as the good old city knew, or any other good old city, town, or borough, in the good old world."

This conclusion to the story finds us coming to the most frightful of realizations. This is the point where we figure out exactly who Ebenezer Scrooge is . . . he's us. I'm Ebenezer Scrooge! I'm getting older and more bitter each year. I'm getting tightfisted and more stingy with my smiles and money. I'm humbugging everything from the shoppers, to the sales, to the traffic, to the weather, to my plastic holiday wreath falling to the ground at my feet. But I too have the chance to be redeemed in a single night. I need only the magic of this holiday to work on me. To understand that the sun is coming back since the Winter Solstice took place. That brighter days lie ahead for me too. That I can make a difference in the world around me.

In Dickens's 1865 book, *Our Mutual Friend*, there's an often-quoted line: "No one is useless in this world who lightens the burdens of it for another." That line shows up quite a bit in *The Man Who Invented Christmas*, the 2017 film about Dickens and his *Christmas Carol.* Those words perfectly sum up the takeaway. If you can help, help. It will make you feel good and make for a better world.

If Scrooge can change all in one night, maybe I can too.

ACT THREE

REDEMPTION

21
The End of It

edemption. If we had to sum up all of this Saturnalia-Yule-Solstice-Midwinter-Christmas fuss with one word, it would be *redemption*. I've toiled all year, tending to my myriad responsibilities. Working to pay my bills, take care of my family, and hopefully have just enough left over to spring for that holiday turkey and some gifts for those I love. During that yearlong grind, I get so focused on all of the tasks I must complete that it's easy for me to ignore the plight of others around me. I get selfish.

Yet, as the days grow short, cold, and dark, I'm reminded to pause and take stock. As the dark shadows hide the many monsters waiting to come for me during Midwinter, I can feel that primal fear begin to swell inside of me.

I'm sure there's some person somewhere who can wake up on any given day and change themselves. Find redemption just because it's logical to do so. But I've never met that person. For the rest of us, it often takes a frightful event to trigger this metamorphosis. A heart attack that we survive, a near-fatal accident, losing a loved one way too soon, or some other scare that forces us to face our mortality before we are ready. Those events can make us into different people overnight. But so too can this holiday.

If we let the fear do its noble work, there's a chance we too can change in a single night. There's still magic in this holiday. A holiday we get to redefine every year. We carry forward traditions that work for us, we can adopt new ideas and practices that feel right, and we can change. It's not too late.

If you want to make this holiday about celebrating the birth of Jesus and everything he stood for, you can! For plenty, this is a deeply religious holiday (and the only day of the year that some go to church). But long before the birth of Jesus, this holiday was secular. It was inclusive of all people, because the Winter Solstice affects all people, no matter what belief system you subscribe to, or even if you believe in no religion at all. Frigid temperatures and short days affect everyone who lives in colder climates. We can't face down winter's icy hand alone. We're going to need each other to get through to the other side. If we try to go it alone, the consequences could be dire.

Over the past century, consequences have mostly been removed from this holiday. When I was growing up, the consequence for bad behavior was fewer presents. Or no presents. Or coal and sticks. But I was never in any bodily danger. Krampus, Belsnickel, Grýla, the Tomten, the Karakoncolos, and the other hordes of monsters were not on my childhood radar. Primal fear was not part of my holiday traditions. However, that fear has its place. Those monsters can work magic if we let them. They worked their magic on me as I took a deep dive into this holiday shortly after my Christmas wreath fell to the ground on that cold December day years ago. It didn't matter that I was no longer a child. I'm grateful to know I'm not too old for saving.

Now, when I hang the wreath on my front door each December, it means something to me. I'm hoping those prickly pine needles do indeed keep those bad spirits outside and the good cheer inside. I hang mistletoe and adorn my indoor tree with garland as an offering to the tree more powerful than winter. I warm myself by my fireplace as the spirits howl outside, being chased down during Odin's Wild Hunt. I dress my outdoor bushes with strings of electric lights to illuminate the long, dark nights, because I know tough times are coming. And if your roof collapses under the weight of the snow, I want those lights to serve as a beacon, so you can find my house and know you can take shelter there, because I know you'd do the same for me.

Winter is coming. But the sun will return. While we wait, let's sing and dance, exchange gifts, celebrate what we have, take care of each other, and scare away the ghosts and monsters who hunt us when we're most vulnerable.

Bibliography

Bain, Jennifer. "Newfoundland's Quirky Christmas Mummering Tradition Celebrated with Festival and Parade." *Toronto Star*, 20 December 2017. *www.thestar.com*.

Barone, Fran. "Winter Solstice Celebrations around the World." *Human Relations Area Files*, Yale University, 24 December 2018. *hraf.yale.edu*.

Basu, Tanya, and Becky Little. "Krampus the Christmas Devil Is Coming to More Towns. So Where's He From?" *National Geographic*, 22 December 2014. *www.nationalgeographic.com*.

Blunt, Rev. John James. *Vestiges of Ancient Manners and Customs Discoverable in Modern Italy and Sicily*. London: John Murray, Albemarle-Street, 1823.

Boissoneault, Lorraine. "A Civil War Cartoonist Created the Modern Image of Santa Claus as Union Propaganda." *Smithsonian Magazine*, 19 December 2018. *www.smithsonianmag.com*.

Daley, Jason. "Is This St. Nicolas' Pelvis Bone?" *Smithsonian Magazine*, 8 December 2017. *www.smithsonianmag.com*.

Denova, Rebecca. "Constantine's Conversion to Christianity." *World History Encyclopedia*, 10 May 2021. *www.worldhistory.org*.

Dickens, Charles. *A Christmas Carol: In Prose. Being a Ghost Story of Christmas*. London: Bradbury & Evans, 1858.

Dolby, George. *Charles Dickens as I Knew Him: The Story of the Reading Tours in Great Britain and America*. London: T. Fisher Unwin, 1885.

Elliot, Jock. *Inventing Christmas: How Our Holiday Came to Be*. New York: Harry N. Abrams, Inc., Publishers, 2002.

Evans, Rev. J. *Through Part of North Wales: In the Year 1798, and at Other Times.* London: J. White, 1800.

Griffin, Emma. *Liberty's Dawn: A People's History of the Industrial Revolution.* New Haven and London: Yale University Press, 2013.

Gunnell, Terry. "Jól in Iceland." National Museum, Reykjavík, 20 December 2008, presentation.

Huxtable, Sally-Anne. "Ritual and Revelry, the Story of Wassailing." *National Trust,* 13 December 2019. *www.nationaltrust.org.uk.*

Irving, Washington. *Knickerbocker's History of New York.* New York: Frederick Ungar Publishing Co., 1928.

Messadié, Gerald. *A History of the Devil.* New York: Kodansha International, 1997.

Montesano, Marina. "Horns, Hooves and Hell: The Devil in Medieval Times." *National Geographic,* 2 November 2018. *www.nationalgeographic.co.uk.*

Neutkens, Susanne. "Het eerste Sinterklaasboek." *Historiën,* 17 November 2018. *www.historien.nl.*

Nissenbaum, Stephen. *The Battle for Christmas: A Cultural History of America's Most Cherished Holiday.* New York: Vintage Books, 1996.

Nuss, Pierre. "Le Hans Trapp a-t-il vraiment existé en Alsace?" *France Bleu Elsass,* 6 December 2021. *www.francebleu.fr.*

Nuwer, Rachel. "Meet the Thirteen Yule Lads, Iceland's Own Mischievous Santa Clauses." *Smithsonian Magazine,* 17 December 2013. *www.smithsonianmag.com.*

Raedisch, Linda. *The Old Magic of Christmas: Yuletide Traditions for the Darkest Days of the Year.* Woodbury, MN: Llewellyn Publications, 2013.

Ridenour, Al. *The Krampus: And the Old, Dark, Christmas Roots and Rebirth of the Folkloric Devil.* Port Townsend, WA: Feral House, 2016.

Rogers, Jude. "The Midwinter Majesty of the Mari Lwyd." Wales.com, 13 December 2019. *www.wales.com*.

Smith, William. *Dictionary of Greek and Roman Biography and Mythology*. London: Taylor, Walton, and Maberly, 1870.

Stearns, Peter N. *The Industrial Revolution in World History: Third Edition*. Boulder, CO: Westview Press, 2007.

Stevens, Patricia Bunning. *Merry Christmas: A History of the Holiday*. New York: Macmillan Publishing Co., 1979.

Walter, Philippe. *Christian Mythology: Revelations of Pagan Origins*. Rochester, VT: Inner Traditions, 2006.

Weightman, Gavin. *The Industrial Revolutionaries: The Making of the Modern World, 1776–1914*. New York: Grove Press, 2007.

Art Credits

Original illustrations by T. Reed © 2023. Reuse prohibited without permission from the publisher.

Emperor Constantine and the Council of Nicaea. From MS CLXV, *Biblioteca Capitolare*, Vercelli, a compendium of canon law produced in northern Italy ca. 825. James Steakley; artwork: unknown, public domain, via Wikimedia Commons.

A 17th-century oil painting by Jan van Dalen depicting the Roman god of wine Bacchus (Kunsthistorisches Museum, Vienna). Jan van Dalen, public domain, via Wikimedia Commons.

"Merry Christmas!" from the *Illustrated London News*, December 25, 1847. Kenny Meadows, public domain, via Wikimedia Commons.

Danish boy carrying a church in the bleak landscape. Holiday postcard illustrated by Jenny Nyström, 1910. Jenny Nyström, public domain, via Wikimedia Commons.

From *The Book of Christmas* by Thomas Kibble Hervey, 1836. Illustrated by Robert Seymour (1798–1836). Public domain, via Wikimedia Commons.

Adam Wcislek with the Krampus mask he commissioned from Stefan Koidl of Hallein, Austria. Photo used by permission of Adam Wcislek.

Saint Nicholas and his companion Knecht Ruprecht knocking on the window, illustration, late 19th century, Germany. INTERFOTO / Alamy Stock Photo.

"The Wassail Bowl at Christmas." English illustration, 1860. World History Archive / Alamy Stock Photo.

"The unique New Year's Festival in Philadelphia—A procession of Masqueraders passing the Post-Office," December 1892. Historical Society of Pennsylvania print collection. Used by permission.

Åsgårdsreien, by Peter Nicolai Arbo, 1872. National Gallery of Norway. Public domain, via Wikimedia Commons.

Mari Lwyd, © Kim Thompson. See Kim Thompson on Instagram: @kim_a_tron, Facebook: Kim Thompson Illustration, and Etsy: Kim Thompson Art.

Yule Cat, © Kim Thompson. See Kim Thompson on Instagram: @kim_a_tron, Facebook: Kim Thompson Illustration, and Etsy: Kim Thompson Art.

Christmas card, 1899, by Jenny Nyström, showing the *jultomten* she popularized. National Library of Norway. Jenny Nyström, public domain, via Wikimedia Commons.

The Tomten enjoying their bowls of risgrynsgröt. Illustration by Jenny Nyström, c. 1900. Public domain, via Wikimedia Commons.

"Hans Trapp accompanies the Christmas Maiden." Hand-colored woodcut of a 19th-century illustration. North Wind Picture Archives / Alamy Stock Photo.

The cover of *Sint Nikolaas en Zijn Knecht (Saint Nicholas and His Servant)*, by Jan Schenkman, 1850, Amsterdam. Illustrator unknown. Public domain, via Wikimedia Commons.

"Sinterclaus keeps a book," an illustration from *Sint Nikolaas en Zijn Knecht (Saint Nicholas and His Servant)*, by Jan Schenkman, 1850, Amsterdam. Illustrator unknown. Public domain, via Wikimedia Commons.

Zwarte Piet, stuffing the bad children into a sack. An illustration from *Sint Nikolaas en Zijn Knecht* by Jan Schenkman, 1850, Amsterdam. Public domain, via Wikimedia Commons.

Strenua. Roma, ca. 400. Photograph from Hayford Pierce and Royal Tyler, *L'art byzantin*, Paris, 1932. Public domain, via Wikimedia Commons.

La Befana, by Bartolomeo Pinelli, 1821. Gift of Ruth Cole Kainen. This file was donated to Wikimedia Commons as part of a project by the National Gallery of Art.

St. Nicholas, by John Pintard, 1810. Woodcut by Alexander Anderson (1775-1870), verse by John Pintard (1759-1844). Credit: New York Historical Society for the public domain, via Wikimedia Commons.

Santa, by Thomas Nast, 1863, for *Harper's Weekly*. Thomas Nast, public domain, via Wikimedia Commons.

Merry Old Santa Claus, by Thomas Nast, 1881. Thomas Nast, public domain, via Wikimedia Commons.

"My Hat's Off to the Pause that Refreshes," by Haddon Sundblom, the *Saturday Evening Post*, 1931. First Sundblom Santa, My Hat's Off, print ad © 1931 The Coca-Cola Company. Used by permission.

"Marley's ghost," an illustration from Charles Dickens, *A Christmas Carol. In Prose. Being a Ghost Story of Christmas*. With illustrations by John Leech. London: Chapman & Hall, 1843. First edition. John Leech, public domain, via Wikimedia Commons.

"The Ghost of Christmas Present," an illustration from Charles Dickens, *A Christmas Carol. In Prose. Being a Ghost Story of Christmas*. With illustrations by John Leech. London: Chapman & Hall, 1843. First edition. John Leech, public domain, via Wikimedia Commons.

"The Ghost of Christmas Yet to Come," an illustration from Charles Dickens, *A Christmas Carol. In Prose. Being a Ghost Story of Christmas*. With illustrations by John Leech. London: Chapman & Hall, 1843. First edition. John Leech, public domain, via Wikimedia Commons.

About the Author

eff Belanger is one of the most visible and prolific research-ers of legends and lore today. A natural storyteller, he's the award-winning, Emmy-nominated host, writer, and producer of the *New England Legends* series on PBS and Amazon Prime, and he hosts the award-winning *New England Legends* weekly podcast.

Always one for chasing adventures, Jeff has climbed Mt. Kilimanjaro in Africa, explored the ruins of Machu Picchu in Peru, and searched the catacombs of Paris, France (where he encountered his first ghost). He faced his lifelong struggle with basophobia on his birthday by skydiving, and he's been ghost hunting all over the world, from a former TB asylum in Kentucky, to medieval castles in Europe, to an abandoned prison in Australia.

His books include: *The World's Most Haunted Places*, *Weird Massachusetts*, *Our Haunted Lives*, and his memoir, *The Call of Kilimanjaro*. A noted public speaker and media personality, he was featured in the hundredth episode of *Stories from the Stage* on PBS, he's given a TEDx talk in New York City, and he spoke at MENSA's national conference. Belanger has written for newspapers like *The Boston Globe* and *USA Today*, and he has served as a writer and researcher on numerous television series, including every epi-sode of *Ghost Adventures* on Travel Channel and Discovery+. He's been featured on camera as an expert and investigator on the *Shock Docs* series

The author and Yuletide friends at the 2022 Krampus Ball.
Photograph by Frank Grace.

on Travel Channel and Discovery+, and he's been a guest on hundreds of radio, podcast, and television networks and programs, including: History Channel, Travel Channel, Biography Channel (now FYI), Reelz, PBS, NECN, Living TV (UK), Sunrise 7 (Australia), the CBS News *Early Show*, *CBS Sunday Morning*, FOX, NBC, ABC, and CBS affiliates, National Public Radio, the BBC, Australian Radio Network, and *Coast to Coast AM*.